HOW TO
THINK LIKE
OBAMA

HOW TO
THINK LIKE
OBAMA

DANIEL SMITH

Michael O'Mara Books Limited

For Charlotte and Ben

First published in Great Britain in 2018 by
Michael O'Mara Books Limited
9 Lion Yard
Tremadoc Road
London SW4 7NQ

A CIP catalogue record for this book is available from the British Library.

Papers used by Michael O'Mara Books Limited are natural, recyclable
products made from wood grown in sustainable forests. The manufacturing
processes conform to the environmental regulations of the country of origin.

ISBN: 978-1-78243-994-3 in hardback print format
ISBN: 978-1-78929-003-5 in paperback print format
ISBN: 978-1-78929-001-1 in ebook format

1 3 5 7 9 10 8 6 4 2

Designed and typeset by Envy Design Ltd

Printed and bound by CPI Group (UK) Ltd, Croydon, CR0 4YY

www.mombooks.com

Contents

Introduction

'It felt like a new day.'

OPRAH WINFREY IN 'MAN OF THE MOMENT'

AT OPRAH.COM, 2005

Barack Obama's place in history is assured as the first African-American man to hold the office of President of the United States. That fact alone marks him out as one of the most significant people of our age. Yet, there is much more to his story that is sometimes at risk of being lost behind that single accolade.

Emerging from a sometimes troubled and disrupted childhood, he initially entered the wider public consciousness as the first African-American chairman of the renowned *Harvard Law Review*. From there, he launched a literary career with a memoir considered something of a contemporary masterpiece. All this all before his political career had taken wing.

As he embarked upon the search for public office, he confounded the odds again. From the Illinois State Senate he moved to the federal Senate – only the fifth African American to do so and, aged just forty-three, one of the youngest, too. By then he had come to national attention after delivering one of the great speeches of the modern age at the National Democratic Convention in 2004. It paved the way for his march to the White House in 2008, when he overcame criticisms that he was too young and inexperienced to become the most powerful individual in the world. He, needless to say, also had to contend with that part of the political firmament which was simply not ready to see a person of colour in the Oval Office.

He came to office riding a wave of popular optimism. As the Nobel Prize Committee would note when awarding him their honour in 2009:

> Only very rarely has a person to the same extent as Obama captured the world's attention and given its people hope for a better future. His diplomacy is founded in the concept that those who are to lead the world must do so on the basis of values and attitudes that are shared by the majority of the world's population. For 108 years, the Norwegian Nobel Committee has sought to stimulate precisely that international policy and those attitudes for which Obama is now the world's leading spokesman. The Committee endorses Obama's appeal that 'Now is the time for all of us to take our share of responsibility for a global response to global challenges.'

If Obama thought getting to the White House would be the really hard bit, the realities of the presidency soon disavowed him of such a notion. He took office as the US economy was failing and found himself at the centre of an international scene increasingly destabilized in the face of regional unrest in North Africa and the Middle

East, accelerating Russian aggression and the rise of utterly brutal new terrorist organizations.

Some of those who had questioned his suitability for the job rubbed their hands with glee. Elizabeth Cheney, a politician and daughter of George W. Bush's vice president Dick Cheney, would, for example, comment in 2010: 'A gift for reading from a teleprompter is not the same as leadership.' And in 2013, the Republican Governor of New Jersey, Chris Christie, described him as being 'more concerned about being right than he is concerned about getting things done'.

It is true that Obama's idealism and intellectualism (strikingly at odds with the down-home style of his predecessor and the bombast of his successor) was often a source of frustration for his critics. For his supporters, though, it has been a vital aspect of his appeal. In 2009, *The New York Times'* columnist David Brooks said of him:

> Whatever policy differences people may have with him, we can all agree that he exemplifies reticence, dispassion and the other traits associated with dignity. The cultural effects of his presidency are not yet clear, but they may surpass his policy impact. He may revitalize the concept of dignity for a new generation and embody a new set of rules for self-mastery.

It is too soon to say how successful or not his presidency was. There are successes and failures to be assessed on both sides of the scale. Domestically, he was often tied by the grim prevailing economic conditions and by a Republican-dominated Congress unwilling to deal with him. Yet there were notable successes – for instance, he pushed through the most radical reforms to healthcare in decades and managed a path through the financial crisis. Internationally, he pursued a less hawkish regime than that inherited from George W. Bush and could point to the capture and elimination of Osama bin Laden as a highlight, along with improving relations with Cuba and Iran. Moreover, he did much to further the cause of global environmentalism. Nonetheless, he was to a degree blindsided by events in the Middle East – especially Syria – and was unable to usher in the era of greater international harmony that his Nobel Prize had seemed to promise.

Nonetheless, Obama has begun the transition from political figure to cultural icon – a path trodden by the likes of Martin Luther King, Mahatma Gandhi and Nelson Mandela, all of whom Obama has taken inspiration from. Even as his reputation continues to be battered by domestic opponents, on the international stage he is held in high esteem. His considered manner, progressive liberalism, and advocacy for social and economic equality resonate powerfully, as does his doctrine of international cooperation. Moreover, his consistent composure amid the gloves-off atmosphere of Washington politics sets him apart. But like Mandela, it may be that his voice is most powerful when unshackled from the day-to-day duties of high office.

Throughout his career, Obama has stayed true to

his core principles. He values fairness and equality of opportunity and, for his supporters at least, embodies a brand of compassionate liberalism that is not always to the fore in public life. This book attempts to look at the philosophies and ideas that have guided him, along with the circumstances and events that helped mould him. It seeks to explore Obama as both a public figure and a private individual. Revealed is a man who has been driven by exceptional optimism – optimism that he also inspires in others. He emerges as uncommonly resilient, too, tough even as he is compassionate, determined even as he accepts the need to compromise. Wherever you stand in relation to him on the political spectrum, his is one of the great lives of modern times.

As the Icelandic prime minister, Lars Løkke Rasmussen, commented of him in 2016: 'Well, being a role model is not always easy, so I've heard. But you, Mr President, have come to represent a dream for millions of Americans and people across the world.'

Landmarks in a Remarkable Life

1961   Barack Hussein Obama Jr is born on 4 August in Hawaii. His parents are Ann Dunham, a white American, and Barack Obama Sr, a Kenyan national.

1962   Barack Obama Sr earns a graduate scholarship to Harvard and relocates to Boston.

1963   Ann returns to her studies, and her parents assist in bringing up Barack.

1964   Dunham files for divorce and begins dating an Indonesian fellow student, Lolo Soetoro.

1965   Barack Obama Sr returns to Kenya. Dunham marries Soetoro.

1967   Dunham and Barack Jr join Soetoro in Jakarta, Indonesia.

1970   Dunham gives birth to Maya Soetoro, Obama's half-sister.

1971   Dunham sends Obama back to Hawaii to live

with her parents and to be educated in America. He enrols at the private Punahou School.

1972   Dunham leaves her husband to return to Hawaii with Maya. Obama Sr visits from Kenya. It is the last time father and son will see each other.

1979   Obama graduates from high school and enrols at Occidental College in Los Angeles.

1980   Dunham files for divorce from Lolo Seotoro.

1981   Obama transfers from Occidental to New York's Columbia University.

1982   Obama Sr is killed in a car crash.

1983   Obama graduates.

1983–7 He remains in New York for a spell before becoming a community organizer with the Developing Communities Project in Chicago. He also wins a place at Harvard Law School.

1987   Obama visits Kenya.

1988   He undertakes his studies at Harvard.

1989   Obama meets Michelle Robinson when she is chosen to mentor him during an internship at Chicago's Sidley & Austin law firm.

1990   He is chosen as the first African-American president of the *Harvard Law Review*.

1991   He graduates from Harvard (*Juris Doctor magna cum laude*) and signs a publishing deal to write a memoir, *Dreams From My Father*.

1992   He begins legal practice in Chicago, specializing in civil rights, and teaches constitutional law at the University of Chicago Law School.

Obama marries Michelle Robinson. He also becomes director of Illinois Project Vote, aimed at registering minority voters. Obama registers approximately 100,000 new voters, primarily in the African-American community.

1995   *Dreams From My Father* is published.

1996   Obama wins a seat in the Illinois State Senate as a Democrat.

1998   Michelle gives birth to a daughter, Malia Ann. Her husband is re-elected to the State Senate.

2000   He unsuccessfully runs for Congress.

2001   Michelle has a second daughter, Natasha (known as Sasha).

2002   Obama is re-elected to the State Senate.

2003   He becomes chair of the Senate's Health and Human Services Committee.

2004   He runs for the US Senate, having won the Illinois Democratic primaries. In July he gives the keynote address at the National Democratic Convention. His speech, known as 'The Audacity of Hope', receives widespread coverage. In November he is elected to the US Senate with 70 per cent of the vote, so becoming only the fifth African American to enter the Senate.

2006   *The Audacity of Hope* is published.

2007   Obama announces his candidacy for the presidency ahead of the 2008 election.

2008   He defeats the heavily fancied former First Lady, Hillary Clinton, to win the Democratic

	nomination and then defeats the Republican candidate, John McCain, to become the nation's first African-American president.
2009	He is sworn in as the country's forty-fourth president. Among his first acts is to sign an economic stimulus bill worth over US$700 billion. Later in the year, he is awarded the Nobel Prize for Peace.
2010	He signs the Patient Protection and Affordable Care Act (known as Obamacare) into law and introduces new financial regulation. After mid-term elections, the Republicans take control of the House of Representatives.
2011	Obama announces he will stand for re-election. Also, US special forces track down and kill Osama bin Laden in Pakistan.
2012	Obama defeats Republican Mitt Romney to claim a second term as president. In a school shooting at Sandy Hook at the end of the year, twenty six- and seven-year-olds are murdered, along with six members of staff. Internationally, the US consulate and annex in Benghazi (Libya) are attacked by militants and the ambassador is killed.
2013	Obama is sworn in for his second term. Terrorists launch a bomb attack on the Boston Marathon.
2014	US forces carry out air strikes in Syria. Obama announces the normalization of relations with Cuba.
2015	The Republicans become the majority party in

both houses of Congress. Obama announces an international deal with Iran to curb its nuclear activities. He also speaks at the United Nations (UN) Climate Change Conference in Paris ahead of the adoption of a major new international agreement on regulating carbon emissions.

2016   Obama gives his backing to Hillary Clinton as the Democratic nominee for the presidency. He labels Republican nominee Donald Trump as a 'home-grown demagogue' and 'unfit to hold office'. Nonetheless, Trump wins the presidency.

2017   Obama leaves the White House. Penguin Random House announces a US$65 million book deal with the Obamas. Obama also outlines his plans for the Obama Presidential Center in Chicago, which is described as a 'campus for active citizenship'.

2018   Netflix announces a deal with the Obamas to produce programmes and movies over several years.

Everything Starts with Family

'Of all the rocks upon which we build
our lives, we are reminded today that family
is the most important.'

BARACK OBAMA, 2008

Barack Obama's start in life was anything but traditional. When he was born on 4 August 1961 in Honolulu, the capital of the island state of Hawaii, nobody could have seriously predicted that the White House would loom in his future. Yet for all of its unorthodoxy, Obama's family would instil in him the principles and ambition that saw him rise to high office.

The roll call of American presidents had, until Obama, been united by certain characteristics – most obviously, their maleness and whiteness. Moreover, more often than not they came from prosperous families, often boasting a long heritage. Apart from being born male, Obama's story started noticeably differently.

His mother, Ann Dunham, was a white teenager when she gave birth to him, and his father (also called Barack Obama) was a student economist who hailed from Kenya. In his memoir, *Dreams From My Father*, the younger Obama would say: 'That my father looked nothing like the people around me – that he was black as pitch, my mother white as milk – barely registered in my mind.' But if he was colour-blind, much of the rest of the population was not so progressive. This was, after all, a time when interracial marriage was still illegal in some states.

His parents had met only the year before his birth while both studying at the University of Hawaii, Obama Sr having won a prestigious scholarship for foreign students. They married in February 1961 and subsequently named their child Barack – 'blessed' in Swahili – although he soon became known as Barry. Within a few weeks of his birth, Obama's mother moved herself and her young son to Seattle, where she studied at the University of Washington. Obama Sr stayed in Hawaii until 1962 when he graduated in economics. He then began a master's degree at Harvard, living separately from the rest of the family. In 1964, the Obama marriage conclusively fell apart and the following year Obama Sr went back to Kenya, where he remarried. Barack would be ten years old before father and son saw each other again.

Dunham, meanwhile, remarried in 1965, having fallen in love with another fellow student – an Indonesian called Lolo Soetoro. He returned to Indonesia the following year, with his wife and stepchild joining him in 1967. Obama spent the next four years being schooled in Jakarta (including a period of home-schooling with his mother) during which time he kept a monkey as a pet and also became fluent in Indonesian. It was around this time that he first gave voice to his ambitions to one day be American president. Moreover, he learned to box (under the tutelage of Soetoro), having been preyed upon by some local bullies. His efforts at the 'sweet science' no doubt provided him with useful skills for his later dealings with Congress.

THE REALITIES OF LIFE

In the US, the civil rights movement was gathering a head of steam. The Civil Rights Act of 1964 outlawed many forms of discrimination, including those based on race or colour, while the Voting Rights Act of the following year sought to end prohibitions on African-American voting rights at the state and local level. His mother encouraged Barack's interest in the rapidly developing social climate back in the US, while also pushing his mastery of English, and gradually the young boy's understanding of what it meant to be black in America grew.

Dunham was keen that her son should continue his education in the US, and so sent Barack to a renowned Hawaiian private school, Punahou, when he was ten. His mother, and a half-sister called Maya who was born in 1970, remained in Indonesia while he lived with his maternal grandparents, whom he knew as Toot and Gramps. More upheaval was around the corner, though. His mother's second marriage failed and she returned to Hawaii with Maya in 1972. Barack went to live with them while their mother continued her studies in anthropology. But in 1975 Dunham went back to Indonesia to carry out fieldwork for her PhD, taking Maya with her. Barack, though, did not want to go, so he moved back in with Toot and Gramps and stayed until he graduated from Punahou in 1979.

Obama's youth, then, was marked by repeated disruptions. His struggle to establish a sense of self-identity was heightened by the absence of a consistent father figure. He keenly felt the lack of a relationship with his natural father, whom he wished might serve as a guide and role model. As he would reflect in *Dreams From My Father*, 'There was only one problem: my father was missing. He had left paradise, and nothing that my mother or grandparents told me would obviate that single, unassailable fact.' Yet, where others might have gone off the rails altogether, Obama managed to maintain an admirable sense of equilibrium – although not without the odd outbreak of wayward behaviour, as detailed in the sections to come.

Key to his success in the face of challenges under which others might have crumbled was the remarkable relationship he maintained with his mother, even as they lived thousands of miles apart. A teacher herself, she had striven to ensure he received the best education she could get him, and instilled in him many of the liberal, humanitarian principles that would guide his later political philosophy – including an openness to people of all backgrounds and a willingness to embrace different cultures. She was, he said, again in his book, 'the kindest, most generous spirit I have ever known, and … what is best in me I owe to her'.

Also of vital importance in bolstering him in sometimes torrid times were his beloved maternal grandparents, who offered him home and sanctuary – as well as advice and direction – whenever he needed it. He acknowledged his debt to them in a speech he gave in Houston in February 2018: 'You know, I was born to a teenage mother. My father left when I was two. So I was raised by a single mom and my grandparents. And they didn't have money, and they didn't have fame. What they could give me was love, they gave me an education, and they gave me hope.' It was that love and sense of hope that proved the wellspring from which all his remarkable accomplishments would subsequently emerge.

You Can See a Lot from the Outside Looking In

'As a teen, I had this divided identity …'

BARACK OBAMA, INTERVIEW WITH

O, THE OPRAH MAGAZINE, 2004

One result of Obama's unconventional upbringing was that he was often cast as an outsider – a position that fundamentally moulded his world view. As his sense grew of a world divided along lines of 'them' and 'us', it fostered his belief that true power and change occur when people are brought together. But regularly finding himself on the outside and a step removed from the heart of things also taught him skills of analysing from a distance – attributes he carried into his political life. Having been compelled to consider many aspects of his society from an outsider's position, he brought into his political life an ability to look at problems from afar and with a clear, analytical mind. He has been accused by his critics over the years of being distant and aloof, but it is perhaps more a reflection of a childhood in which he was so often excluded from the mainstream of society.

The fact of his mixed-race heritage ensured his outsider status from the moment of his birth. Born at a moment when the US was re-examining its racial boundaries, often in an explosive and violent atmosphere, the fact of having one white and one black parent set him apart. His mother could claim English, Scottish, Irish, Welsh, German and Swiss roots, while his father's heritage was, of course,

African. Family gatherings, Obama recalled in a speech in Shanghai in 2009, looked 'like the United Nations'. With his dark skin and distinctive name, Obama was treated by the world at large as a black child, with little recognition given to the fact that his upbringing was more influenced by his white relatives. Reconciling his domestic reality with how the outside world saw him was a process that would take him many years.

His outsider status was further consolidated by the gender disparity in his home life. Effectively without a father figure for most of his upbringing (save for the constancy of his grandfather), Obama was brought up in a predominantly feminine environment. He has been unequivocal about the debt he owes to the women in his life, as when he wrote in his 2006 book, *The Audacity of Hope*:

> It was women, then, who provided the ballast in my life – my grandmother, whose dogged practicality kept the family afloat, and my mother whose love and clarity of spirit kept my sisters and my world centred. Because of them I never wanted for anything important. From them I would absorb the values that guide me to this day.

Yet for all that they helped him become the man he did, the pain of the absence of his father is palpable. Obama Sr, his son said, 'remained a myth to me, both more and less than a man'. Obama's route to manhood was undoubtedly rockier for his lack of exposure to traditional adult-male role models.

The cycle of moving home – from Hawaii to Seattle, then to the unfamiliar environs of Jakarta, back to Hawaii and the grandparental home, then living with his mother and sister before once more moving in with Toot and Gramps when mother and sister returned to Indonesia – further added to Obama's sense that he was on the outside looking in. A certain sense of dislocation was unavoidable, even as Obama developed relationship-making skills and a talent for building a life wherever he found himself. Hawaii at least offered a conducive environment for the outsider. Writing in 1999 for the *Punahou Bulletin*, Obama suggested the state offered the chance to experience a variety of cultures in a climate of mutual respect, which 'became an integral part of my world view, and a basis for the values that I hold most dear'.

Nonetheless, life was not easy for Obama, the mixed-race teenager who lived with his grandparents, when he began his studies at the prestigious Punahou School. One of only two black children in the school and with a name that was bound to mark him out, he was once again set apart from the majority. Although he would ultimately carve out a place for himself there, he wrestled with how he fitted into society. Speaking to *O, The Oprah Magazine* in 2004, he said:

As a teen, I had this divided identity – one inside the home, one for the outside world. It wasn't until I got to college that I started realizing that was fundamentally dishonest. I knew there had to be a different way for me to understand myself as a black man and yet not reject the love and values given to me by my mother and her parents. I had to reconcile that I could be proud of my African-American heritage and yet not be limited by it.

Obama would twice win the presidency, claiming the popular vote on each occasion. To that extent, it might be said that the born outsider found the ultimate way to get on the inside. Yet his opponents would repeatedly bring up his non-traditional origins as a stick to beat him with. One need only look to the farcical questioning of whether he could prove he was American-born (see page 211), a required qualification for any presidential candidate. Or consider his words during a speech on the day of the New Hampshire Primary in January 2008: 'At various stages in the campaign, some commentators have deemed me either "too black" or "not black enough".' So often excluded from one social group or another, he learned to straddle multiple worlds with panache. His experience also rendered him sympathetic to the plight of other outsiders. Indeed, in a speech he gave in November 2014, he would suggest America was built upon the shoulders of outsiders:

We didn't raise the Statue of Liberty with her back to the world, we did it with her light shining as a beacon to the world. And whether we were Irish or Italians or Germans crossing the Atlantic, or Japanese or Chinese crossing the Pacific; whether we crossed the Rio Grande or flew here from all over the world – generations of immigrants have made this country into what it is. It's what makes us special.

Be Master of Your Own Identity

'My identity might begin with the fact of my race,
but it didn't, couldn't end there. At least that's what
I would choose to believe.'

BARACK OBAMA, *DREAMS FROM MY FATHER*

In his 2006 book, *The Audacity of Hope*, Obama explained that he cannot help but view the American experience through the prism of a man of mixed heritage, 'forever mindful of how generations of people who looked like me were subjugated and stigmatized, and the subtle and not so subtle ways that race and class continue to shape our lives'. As such, he describes himself as 'a prisoner of my own biography'. Yet this is in certain respects a curious description. Obama has perhaps a greater claim than anyone of his generation to say that he leapt free from the constraints of his own biography. While the facts of that biography – the circumstances of his childhood and the legacy of his mixed-race heritage – have crucially informed his life, by harnessing his talents, ambition and willpower, he has achieved that which his 'biography' seemed to suggest was impossible. Just forty-five years after Martin Luther King talked of his dream of a nation where his children would be judged not by the colour of their skin but by the content of their character, Obama compounded expectations to become the American president. Rather than being a prisoner of his biography, he surely went on to prove that he could be its master.

By embracing his heritage, refusing to be defined by expectations imposed by others, and reaching out across the racial divide that remains a feature of American life, he seized control of his own destiny in the most spectacular way. However, that he would do so was by no means a certainty in his younger days. The mature Obama is the product of a youthful crisis of identity from which he emerged wiser and better equipped to deal with the world.

As a teenager, Obama was able to rely upon his prodigious academic gifts to cruise through school. Speaking to former professional baseball player and now owner of the Miami Marlins, Derek Jeter, in an interview for the *Players' Tribune* in 2016, Obama stated that he would tell his fifteen-year-old self, 'Hit the books and stop goofing off.' He was not, he admitted, a particularly responsible young man, getting by on a mixture of wit and charm and not being very attentive to his schoolwork. He has also conceded he used drugs recreationally in this period, along with a group of friends collectively known as the 'Choom Gang' (choom being a colloquialism for smoking marijuana). When he had the money, he also experimented with cocaine. His reason, he would later reveal in *Dreams From My Father*, was to 'push questions of who I was out of my mind, something that could flatten out the landscape of my heart, blur the edges of my memory'.

Obama struggled to reconcile the different cultural influences that pulled at him. Raised predominantly by a white mother and white grandparents (along with a prolonged period of influence from his Asian stepfather), Obama nonetheless found himself inexorably drawn to his African roots. Yet the one person who could have given some context to that part of his heritage was conspicuous by his absence. Their last meeting was when Barack was ten and Obama Sr visited Hawaii for a month.

Initially, relations between the two – who had not seen each other for some eight years at that stage – were tense. The son resented his father's attempts to impose patriarchal authority. Moreover, the thin, bespectacled figure who walked with a cane thanks to injuries suffered in a car crash hardly fitted the heroic ideal of the young boy's imagination. But as time went on, their bond grew – especially after Obama Sr spoke at Punahou about life in Africa. The son had initially dreaded the event, sure that it would lead to his schoolmates regarding him even more as 'not one of them'. But the talk was a great success. Against expectations, schoolmates told Obama his father was 'cool' and Obama himself saw him in a new light. In their few weeks together, the pair read together and Obama Sr, despite his incapacitation, taught his son some African dance moves.

When Obama Sr returned to Kenya from this short visit, neither knew it would be the last time they would meet. The hold of the father upon the son seemed almost to strengthen as the distance between them and the time since their last meeting grew. The quest to understand how he was shaped by both his experience of white American domestic life and the experiences of his father raised in a tiny Kenyan village gnawed away at Obama. 'It was into my father's image,' he wrote in *Dreams From My Father*, 'the black man, son of Africa, that I'd packed all the attributes I sought in myself.' To be black, he concluded, was to be 'the beneficiary of a great inheritance, a special destiny, glorious burdens that only we were strong enough to bear'. The desire to bring together the disparate fragments of his world burned bright.

At the same time, Obama was becoming increasingly conscious of what the colour of his skin meant in terms of his treatment in the public sphere. In 2013 the killing of an unarmed black youth, Trayvon Martin, at the hands of a local neighbourhood watch volunteer caused ripples through the nation. Obama's comments in the aftermath are instructive as to his own experience of prejudice:

There are very few African American men in this country who haven't had the experience of being followed when they were shopping in a department store. That includes me. There are very few African American men who haven't had the experience of walking across the street and hearing the locks click on the doors of cars. That happens to me – at least before I was a senator. There are very few African Americans who haven't had the experience of getting on an elevator and a woman clutching her purse nervously and holding her breath until she had a chance to get off. That happens often.

Back in 2009 Obama had discussed the potentially debilitating impact of casual prejudice on the black psyche in comments made at the centennial convention of the National Association for the Advancement of Colored People (NAACP). 'One of the most durable and destructive legacies of discrimination,' he said, 'is the way we've internalized a sense of limitation; how so many in our community have come to expect so little from the world and from themselves.' But Obama found the internal resources to buck this trend. First and foremost, he was blessed with significant academic abilities, even if he was not always as dedicated to his studies as he might have wished. As he told the Democratic National Convention in 2012: 'Education was the gateway to opportunity for me.' Moreover, he had an innate sense of ambition. For a while he considered a career as an architect, although it would ultimately be the law and politics that proved the bigger pull. In the end, he did more than enough to get through school, passing his exams and winning a place at Occidental College in Los Angeles in 1979. There he turned from using the name his mother and grandparents had generally called him by, Barry, in favour of his birth name, Barack. It was another attempt to reclaim his identity on his own terms.

By the time he transferred to New York's Columbia University two years later, he was far more at peace with his own identity and imbued with a greater sense of maturity and direction. In part, this was because he had come to realize that he did not want to be defined by expectations

---

NAACP

The National Association for the Advancement of Colored People (NAACP) is an interracial organization opposed to racism in all its forms. Established in 1909 in the aftermath of bloody race riots in Springfield, Illinois, it has been involved in vital legal work over the years, including Brown v. Board of Education of Topeka which resulted in a landmark Supreme Court ruling in 1954 that segregation in public schools was unconstitutional. In 1963 one of its leading activists, Medgar Evers, was murdered by white supremacists in Mississippi. The NAACP was at the forefront of the civil rights movement throughout the 1960s and remains a significant influence in American life. Were it not for the organization's efforts over many decades, it is difficult to see how Obama could have succeeded in his own quest for the White House.

---

imposed upon him on the basis of his skin colour. Even as sections of society attempted to enforce constraints, he was determined to break free of negative expectations and define his own identity. It was an ethos he sought to pass on to a new generation in a speech to students at Howard University in 2016: 'And because you're a black person doing whatever it is that you're doing, that makes it a black thing. Feel confident.'

Your Heritage is Your Context

'The pain I felt was my father's pain.
My questions were my brothers' questions.
Their struggle, my birthright.'

BARACK OBAMA, *DREAMS FROM MY FATHER*

While he was at Columbia, Obama received a letter from his father inviting him to Kenya. It was the first contact between the two for several years. The son was keen to seize the opportunity to get to know his father better, and his mother was also keen that the two should bond. Plans were made that Obama would visit Africa after his graduation. But tragedy struck before he got the opportunity. In 1982, Obama Sr was killed in a traffic accident aged just forty-six.

Nonetheless, Obama eventually made his pilgrimage to Kenya in 1987 and it proved one of the defining experiences of his life. 'Never forget' is an exhortation Obama has used repeatedly in his speeches over the years. Remembering one's history and learning from one's experiences are core tenets of Obama's philosophy. This trip proved a prime opportunity to ensure he connected with his own distinctive familial and cultural history. Where there had hitherto been a yawning gap in his understanding of his own heritage, the journey to Kenya allowed him to fill the vacuum. As he reflected in *Dreams From My Father*:

I realized that who I was, what I cared about, was no longer just a matter of intellect or obligation, no longer a construct of words. I saw that my life in America – the black life, the white life, the sense of abandonment I'd felt as a boy, the frustration and hope I'd witnessed in Chicago – all of it was connected with this small plot of earth an ocean away, connected by more than the accident of a name or the color of my skin.

His father, who had served as an economist in the Kenyan government, was a respected figure in his homeland. By chance, on his arrival in the country Obama Jr encountered a security guard at the airport who knew Obama Sr personally. Such moments gave the son an intense feeling of belonging. Of course, America was home but here was a place where he could be confident that no one would misspell his name or mangle its pronunciation. He had been drawn, he realized, into a network of relationships that he might not yet fully understand but of which he was inextricably a part. 'Welcome home,' an aunt eagerly greeted him, fully aware that he had never before set foot on the continent.

That is not to say, though, that he was able to fully get to the bottom of the enigma that was his father. Three times married, a father several times over (there were at least five children), a Western-educated government man who fell out with President Jomo Kenyatta – he unarguably led a full life. 'Someone once said,' Obama wrote in *The Audacity of Hope*, 'that every man is trying to either live up to his father's expectations or make up for his father's mistakes, and I suppose that may explain my particular malady as well as anything else.' For all his desire to understand his father, his true nature remained elusive. Obama had a go at defining him in a speech at the University of Nairobi in 2006, when he said, 'In many ways, he embodied the new Africa of the early Sixties, a man who had obtained the knowledge of the Western world, and sought to bring it back home, where he hoped he could help create a new nation.' But in certain key respects he remained the 'ghost' with whose image the young Obama had spent his life struggling.

Nonetheless, the trip to Kenya went a long way to helping him reconcile himself with his heritage. He described sitting by his father's grave, crying until the tears gave way to a sense of calmness. 'I felt the circle finally close,' he wrote.

Dare to Dream

'Hope in the face of difficulty, hope in the face of
uncertainty, the audacity of hope.'

BARACK OBAMA, ADDRESS TO THE NATIONAL
DEMOCRATIC CONVENTION, 2004

Alongside natural talent and ambition, another vital component of Obama's road to success – and a key feature of his political life – has been his deep sense of hope. Where others might set aside their dreams as unrealistic or unrealizable, he has tended towards believing that anything is possible – both personally and politically. In his now legendary keynote speech to the National Democratic Convention in 2004, an address commonly known as 'The Audacity of Hope', he said: 'In the end, that is God's greatest gift to us, the bedrock of this nation, a belief in things not seen, a belief that there are better days ahead.'

It is not to go too far to suggest that it was his sense of optimism which propelled him to the White House in 2008. The phrase 'audacity of hope' was actually a corruption of a term used by his then pastor, Jeremiah Wright (see page 162) in a sermon based around George Frederic Watts' painting entitled *Hope*. Obama's own life experience was crucial to giving credence to his suggestion that hope paves the way to a better future. In a speech he gave on the campaign trail in 2008, he laid out a potted version of his biography as a means of illustrating how his story is in essence one of hope overcoming the odds:

> I am the son of a black man from Kenya and a white woman from Kansas. I was raised with the help of a white grandfather who survived a Depression to serve in Patton's army during World War Two and a white grandmother who worked on a bomber assembly line at Fort Leavenworth while he was overseas. I've gone to some of the best schools in America and lived in one of the world's poorest nations. I am married to a black American who carries within her the blood of slaves and slaveowners – an inheritance we pass on to our two precious daughters. I have brothers, sisters, nieces, nephews, uncles and cousins, of every race and every hue, scattered across three continents, and for as long as I live, I will never forget that in no other country on Earth is my story even possible.

But it was that 2004 Democratic National Convention speech that most clearly set out his manifesto of hope – one which posed the critical question: 'Do we participate in a politics of cynicism, or do we participate in a politics of hope?' His was not, he was quick to emphasize, the naïve hope of the incurably romantic, but the realistic hope of the sober rationalist who sees hope as an essential driver of change. He described it as follows:

I'm not talking about blind optimism here, the almost willful ignorance that thinks unemployment will go away if we just don't think about it, or the health care crisis will solve itself if we just ignore it. That's not what I'm talking about. I'm talking about something more substantial. It's the hope of slaves sitting around a fire singing freedom songs; the hope of immigrants setting out for distant shores; the hope of a young naval lieutenant bravely patrolling the Mekong Delta; the hope of a millworker's son who dares to defy the odds; the hope of a skinny kid with a funny name who believes that America has a place for him, too.

He extolled his audience to 'feel the same energy that I do … feel the same urgency that I do … feel the same passion that I do'. It was a message he held to throughout even the darkest moments of his presidential tenure. Take, for example, his words to the National Democratic Convention in 2012, eight years on from the 'Audacity of Hope' address: 'We believe the little girl who's offered an escape from poverty by a great teacher or a grant for college could become the next Steve Jobs or the scientist who cures cancer or the President of the United States, and it is in our power to give her that chance.'

Hope on its own might not be enough, Obama has understood, but hope as part of a cogent plan of government is a powerful force. As Michelle Obama wrote in a letter to the *Advocate* in October 2008: 'Translating hope into action is something Barack has done for his entire life.'

HOPE

In a letter of 1885, George Watts described his subject thus: 'Hope sitting on a globe, with bandaged eyes playing on a lyre which has all the strings broken but one out of which poor little tinkle she is trying to get all the music possible, listening with all her might to the little sound …' The painting – which had earlier inspired a sermon by Martin Luther King Jr and a print of which was said to hang in Nelson Mandela's cell on Robben Island – prompted Obama's pastor, Jeremiah Wright, to talk admiringly of the female subject, dressed in rags and her body bruised and scarred, having the 'audacity to make music and praise God'. 'To take the one string you have left,' he said, 'and to have the audacity to hope … that's the real word God will have us hear from this passage and from Watts' painting.' Such was the potency of Obama's notion of 'the audacity of hope' that it would go on to become the title of his 2006 bestselling book, subtitled 'Thoughts on Reclaiming the American Dream'.

Find Fertile Ground to Grow Your Dream

'That is the true genius of America, a faith … a faith in simple dreams, an insistence on small miracles.'

BARACK OBAMA, ADDRESS TO THE NATIONAL DEMOCRATIC CONVENTION, 2004

'In no other country on Earth is my story even possible,' has been a refrain which has echoed through several of Obama's speeches over the years. It highlights a vital aspect of his particular brand of hope – the conviction that no other nation is so well suited to the fostering of hope and the realization of ambitions. Much of his political capital has rested on his ability to convey a sense of what constitutes the fabled American dream in the contemporary world. His 2006 book, *Audacity of Hope*, may be seen as an extended riff on the concept.

In a speech he gave in Iowa in 2007, Obama spoke of the American dream in these terms: 'Americans share a faith in simple dreams. A job with wages that can support a family. Health care that we can count on and afford. A retirement that is dignified and secure. Education and opportunity for our kids. Common hopes. American dreams.' But where others have traditionally seen the American dream in terms of individualism – the notion that, regardless of the circumstances of birth, an individual might achieve a happy standard of living through hard work – Obama has couched it in terms of a community ideal. As he put it in the 2004 'Audacity of Hope' speech:

> For alongside our famous individualism, there's another ingredient in the American saga, a belief that we are all connected as one people. If there's a child on the south side of Chicago who can't read, that matters to me, even if it's not my child. If there's a senior citizen somewhere who can't pay for their prescription and having to choose between medicine and the rent, that makes my life poorer, even if it's not my grandparent. If there's an Arab-American family being rounded up without benefit of an attorney or due process, that threatens my civil liberties. It is that fundamental belief – I am my brother's keeper, I am my sister's keeper – that makes this country work.

It was an idea he explored further in an interview with the *Chicago Tribune* the same year: 'I have been chasing this same goal my entire adult career, and that is creating an America that is fairer, more compassionate and has greater understanding between its various peoples.' It has been an ongoing concern of his that rising levels of inequality have caused the American dream to slip further from the reach of many poorer Americans striving to join the middle class. While acknowledging that our increasingly globalized economy has given some the opportunity to accumulate unimagined levels of wealth, he feels that a large constituent of people who feel isolated or excluded from the globalization boom have lost faith in the possibility of their own progression.

Obama's goal has been that that sense of optimism for the future can be shared by all regardless of background. That is not to say that he believes the 'dream' can be achieved without toil and effort. In fact, he regards those things as crucial aspects of it. Rather, he believes it 'un-American' where people are deprived of the hope of progression before they have had the chance to make it happen for themselves. As he told his Iowan audience in 2007:

> When our fellow Americans are denied the American dream, our own dreams are diminished … But the politics of hope doesn't mean hoping that things come easy. It's a politics of believing in things unseen; of believing in what this country might be; and of standing up for that belief and fighting for it when it's hard. America is the sum of our dreams. And what binds us together, what makes us one American family, is that we stand up and fight for each other's dreams … It's time to do that once more. It's time to reclaim the American dream.

As he put it when speaking at the White House in 2015 on the occasion of the Supreme Court ruling in favour of marriage equality for same-sex couples: 'America is a place where you can write your own destiny.' And expanding on the subject in his State of the Union address a year later, he said: 'That's the America I know. That's the country we love. Clear-eyed. Big-hearted. Undaunted by challenge. Optimistic that unarmed truth and unconditional love will have the final word. That's what makes me so hopeful about our future.'

THE AMERICAN DREAM

The American dream may be thought of in terms of each individual's opportunity to pursue their own interpretation of happiness. Typically, this has translated into the wish to have a job which pays enough to sustain a family and enjoy a decent standard of living. It is a concept enshrined in the US Declaration of Independence, which asserts that 'all men are created equal' and are 'endowed by their Creator with certain unalienable Rights, that among these are Life, Liberty and the pursuit of Happiness'. It is implicit that the interests of the whole are best served by allowing each individual the freedom to improve his own lot – and, moreover, to do so under the protection of the law (as long as by doing so, the individual doesn't directly impinge upon the rights of others). The phrase came into popular usage after James Truslow Adams used it in his 1931 work, *Epic of America*. 'The American Dream,' he wrote, 'is that dream of a land in which life should be better and richer and fuller for everyone, with opportunity for each according to ability or achievement.'

Be the Change You Seek

'We, the people, hold in our hands the power to choose our leaders and change our law, and shape our own destiny.'

BARACK OBAMA, 2010

By the time he embarked on his studies at Occidental College, Obama was making significant progress towards resolving many of his issues of personal identity. Now he also began to address the question of how best he could practically realize his dreams and ambitions – for himself and for wider society. It marked the beginning of his formal engagement with the world of politics. Immersed in Occidental's liberal arts culture, he made his first political speech in early 1981, arguing that the college should stop its South African-related investments. At the time, South Africa operated a ruthless apartheid regime and was subject to wide-ranging international sanctions. His speech was the first indication that Obama perceived himself as an agent of change.

Later that year, he transferred to Columbia University, where he majored in political science with a speciality in international relations and English literature. Graduating in 1983, he stayed in New York for a further two years, working as variously a financial researcher and writer, and as a project manager at the non-partisan New York Public Interest Research Group. He increasingly had the sense that he needed to put his money where his mouth was. It was all well and good thinking and talking about the problems he saw around him, but what could he actually do to solve them? He took the momentous decision to relocate to Chicago and start working as a community organizer for a church-based organization called Developing Community Projects.

In this role, he became active in a variety of schemes including preparing people for college and work and representing tenants in disputes with their landlords. One such episode involved him bringing a group of tenants together to challenge their landlord over the results of asbestos tests he claimed to have carried out. Fearing exposure in the press that he had not in fact undertaken any such tests, the landlord immediately commissioned the work and when asbestos was found, the tenants were able to access funds to rectify the problem. This was the sort of real-world change Obama was eager to initiate – and he saw that the quickest way to get results was to bring people with common interests together to work as one. He continued this community work until 1988, when he began his studies at Harvard Law School. A well-trodden path by politicians over the years, it was also indicative of Obama's belief that the most effective way to achieve real change is to reform the law.

It is a theme he would touch upon many years later, in an address to students at Howard University in 2016. On that occasion, he warned his audience – with no shortage of fiery passion – that ordinary people must engage with the political process (most obviously by voting) in order to ensure that the appropriate people are in a position to make the changes they want. 'Even if we dismantled every barrier to voting,' he said, 'that alone would not change the fact that America has some of the lowest voting rates in the free world.' He was speaking at a time when much of his own presidential programme was being constrained by a Republican majority in Congress. He pointed out that:

In 2014, only 36 per cent of Americans turned out to vote in the midterms – the second lowest participation rate on record. Youth turnout – that would be you – was less than 20 per cent. Less than 20 per cent. Four out of five did not vote. In 2012, nearly two in three African Americans turned out. And then, in 2014, only two in five turned out. You don't think that made a difference in terms of the Congress I've got to deal with? And then people are wondering, well, how come Obama hasn't gotten this done? How come he didn't get that done? You don't think that made a difference? What would have happened if you had turned out at 50, 60, 70 per cent, all across this country?

Obama's early career was played out on two fronts – first, by reaching out to people and working directly with them on individual issues, and secondly, by engaging with the law so as to best be able to challenge and change the legal framework that regulates the lives of those ordinary people. At Harvard, he proved a highly talented jurist. He was elected to the prestigious post of editor of the *Harvard*

Law Review, becoming the first African American to hold the post – a fact which earned him significant publicity. Following his graduation in 1991 (magna cum laude) he returned to Chicago – where he had spent his summers interning with various law firms – to lecture at the Chicago Law School and to work as a civil rights attorney. He represented, among others, community organizers, victims of discrimination and black voters striving for the redrawing of city ward boundaries. He was also a leading figure in a voter registration scheme that in the early 1990s succeeded in registering some 150,000 of 400,000 unregistered African Americans in the state of Illinois.

Such successes consolidated his belief that change comes easiest when people come together to work for it. It is a theme he has revisited many times over the years. Take his words delivered on the fiftieth anniversary of the Selma marches (see page 58) in 2015:

> Because Selma shows us that America is not the project of any one person. Because the single most powerful word in our democracy is the word "We." "We The People." "We Shall Overcome." "Yes We Can." That word is owned by no one. It belongs to everyone.'

Or his remarks a year later at the Lyndon B. Johnson Presidential Library Civil Rights Summit in Austin, Texas:

> We shall overcome. We, the citizens of the United States. Like Dr King, like Abraham Lincoln, like countless

citizens who have driven this country inexorably forward, President Johnson knew that ours in the end is a story of optimism, a story of achievement and constant striving that is unique upon this Earth ... He believed that together we can build an America that is more fair, more equal, and more free than the one we inherited. He believed we make our own destiny. And in part because of him, we must believe it as well.

There are other notable examples, too. Back in 2008, at a speech in Philadelphia, he said: 'I believe deeply that we cannot solve the challenges of our time unless we solve them together – unless we perfect our union by understanding that we may have different stories, but we hold common hopes ...' Fast forward to 2015 and it was the legal enshrining of gay marriage that prompted him to observe:

What an extraordinary achievement. What a vindication of the belief that ordinary people can do extraordinary things. What a reminder of what Bobby Kennedy once said about how small actions can be like pebbles being thrown into a still lake, and ripples of hope cascade outwards and change the world.

Obama has more than once over the years referenced Martin Luther King's assertion that 'the arc of the moral universe is long, but it bends towards justice'. 'He's right,' Obama said in 2005, 'but you know what? It doesn't bend on its own. It bends because we help it bend that way.' It is an attitude of mind he arguably most memorably summed up while on the campaign trail in 2008: 'We are the change that we seek.'

THE SELMA TO MONTGOMERY MARCHES

It is possible to trace a clear lineage from Obama back to the civil rights leaders of the 1960s. A pivotal episode from that period – one that profoundly influenced Obama's philosophy of peaceful mass action – was the series of Selma to Montgomery marches that took place in Alabama in March 1965. On Sunday 7th of that month, some 600 people began the 50+-mile march. They were demanding black voting rights but also commemorating Jimmie Lee Jackson, who had been shot dead by a state trooper at a civil rights protest the previous month. The march ended in disarray when television cameras caught clashes with armed police on Edmund Pettus Bridge on the outskirts of Selma. Seventeen people were hospitalized, including the congressman John Lewis (see Obama's Heroes on page 90), in what became known as 'Bloody Sunday'. A further march two weeks later made it all the way to the Capitol building and voting reform followed later in the year. Speaking in 2005, Obama said: '... change is never easy, but always possible ... it comes not from violence or militancy or the kind of politics that pits us against each other and plays on our worst fears; but from great discipline and organization, from a strong message of hope, and from the courage to turn against the tide so that the tide eventually may be turned'.

Behind Every
Great Man …

'She is the smartest, toughest, funniest best
friend that I could ever hope for, and she's always
had my back.'

BARACK OBAMA DISCUSSING MICHELLE OBAMA,
WASHINGTON POST, 2006

Undoubtedly one of the great strengths of the Obama White House was the relationship between President and First Lady. By no means the first First Lady to add positive value to a presidency, Michelle Obama was nonetheless an asset whose value to her husband cannot be underestimated. So much so that when he left office, there were plenty of commentators raising the prospect that she might make her own run for the highest office in the land at some point in the future. (She insists she won't, saying in 2018: 'I've never had the passion for politics. I just happened to be married to somebody who has the passion for politics, and he dragged me kicking and screaming into this arena.')

In Michelle, Obama found someone who was on an intellectual level with him. While their relationship could have become horribly imbalanced as his career took off, it has shown the hallmarks of remaining remarkably stable. This has surely been in no small part down to their shared belief that it is a partnership of equals.

In fact, at its very beginning it was Michelle who arguably held the whip hand. Michelle shares clear parallels with another First Lady of fairly recent vintage, Hillary

Clinton. But where Clinton could be abrasive and became a highly divisive figure, Michelle Obama nurtured a softer image, although that is not to say that she was not sometimes outspoken or that she attempted to disguise her prodigious intellectual capacities.

The Obamas met in the summer of 1989 when Michelle Robinson – a graduate of Princeton and Harvard Law ('I am not a super genius,' she would later say, instead putting her success down to 'that perfect storm of good parents, self-esteem and good teachers') and daughter of an employee of the Chicago water plant department and a stay-at-home mother – was assigned as Obama's mentor at the Chicago law firm, Sidley & Austin, which had agreed to employ him for the summer before he returned to his studies at Harvard. A couple of years younger than him, she was far from overawed by the new boy. Although she acknowledged that there was 'this buzz about this guy', she considered that they probably had little in common as she assumed, somewhat wryly, that 'any black guy who came from Hawaii had to be weird'.

Despite her reluctance, on principle, to become romantically involved with any work colleagues, their relationship nonetheless eventually blossomed and persisted even when they were living in different cities – he in Boston and she in Chicago. They married in 1992. Valerie Jarrett, Michelle's one-time boss, was struck by the partnership element of their marriage. 'I never heard Barack say, "I want to do it. Can you support me?"' she recalled. 'Instead, they both asked themselves, "Does this make sense for us?"' One important decision they made was that Michelle would move out of legal practice to work in the public and voluntary sectors. Among the positions she held were associate dean of Student Services at the University of Chicago and vice president for Community and External Affairs of the University of Chicago Medical Center – senior roles that commanded significant salaries. But when Barack decided to run for the presidency, she cut down her hours to ensure their children received a high level of parental input. It was indicative of how Obama's path up the political ladder always benefited from Michelle's unstinting support.

Pressures Shared are Pressures Halved

'Most people who meet my wife quickly conclude that she is remarkable. They are right about this. She is smart, funny and thoroughly charming. Often, after hearing her speak at some function or working with her on a project, people will approach me and say something to the effect of, you know, I think the world of you, Barack, but your wife, wow!'

BARACK OBAMA, *THE AUDACITY OF HOPE*

Obama has been acutely aware of the pressures that his wife has had to endure as the result of his career choices. In 2016, he told *Glamour* magazine:

> I've seen how Michelle has balanced the demands of a busy career and raising a family. Like many working mothers, she worried about the expectations and judgments of how she should handle the trade-offs, knowing that few people would question my choices. And the reality was that when our girls were young, I was often away from home serving in the state legislature, while also juggling my teaching responsibilities as a law professor. I can look back now and see that, while I helped out, it was usually on my schedule and on my terms. The burden disproportionately and unfairly fell on Michelle.

In that same interview, Obama acknowledged that the most important people in his life have always been women, from his mother and grandmother through to Michelle and his by then grown-up daughters. They have variously shown him qualities of perseverance and selflessness, and he has admired their many achievements – his grandmother working her way up in the banking industry (despite the presence of a definitive glass ceiling), his mother working to empower other women in developing nations, and Michelle's remarkable record of professional accomplishments – achieved even as she supported her husband's move up the political ladder.

In an interview with *Vogue* in 2013, Obama said:

> She is a great mom. What is also true is Michelle's had to accommodate a life that it's fair to say was not necessarily what she envisioned for herself. She has to put up with me. And my schedule and my stresses. And she's done a great job on that. But I think it would be a mistake to think that my wife, when I walk in the door, is, 'Hey, honey, how was your day? Let me give you a neck rub.' It's not as if Michelle is thinking in terms of, 'How do I cater to my husband?' I think it's much more, 'We're a team, and how do I make sure that this guy is together enough that he's paying attention to his girls and not forgetting the basketball game that he's supposed to be going to on Sunday?' So, she's basically managing me quite effectively.

But her role goes beyond mere logistical planning. She offers Obama emotional succour too. 'Obviously I couldn't have done anything that I've done without Michelle,' he told Oprah Winfrey in 2011. 'You were asking earlier what keeps me sane, what keeps me balanced, what allows me to deal with the pressure. It is this young lady right here … Not only has she been a great first lady, she is just my rock. I count on her in so many ways every single day.' That she offers him a refuge from the day-to-day pressures of life in Washington DC was a subject he had previously covered with *The New York Times* in 2009. 'What I value most about my marriage,' he said then, 'is that it is separate and apart from a lot of the silliness of Washington. And Michelle is not part of that silliness.'

Thrust into the spotlight as First Lady and compelled, whether she liked it or not, to take on a public persona, she inhabited the role with great poise. Fortunately, she is blessed with a level of self-confidence undoubtedly vital to prosper in the role. It was a quality evident in a speech she gave in 2007:

Funny thing, the more I achieved, the more I found that I was just as ready, just as qualified, just as capable as those who felt entitled to the seat at the table that I was working so hard for. And I realized that those who had been given the mantle of power in this country didn't have any magic about them. They were no better, no smarter than me. That gnawing sense of self-doubt that is common within all of us is a lie. It's just in our heads. Nine times out of ten, we are more ready and more prepared than we could ever know.

She managed to convey a sense of ease whether mixing with world leaders, school children or pop stars. Obama's tenure in the White House coincided with the reign of Jay-Z and Beyoncé as America's pre-eminent entertainment power-couple, and Barack and Michelle Obama brought a similar kind of stardust to the political firmament. That image was helped by Michelle's sense of sartorial style – she has often been likened to Jacqueline Kennedy, wife of John F. Kennedy, for her ability to be at once fashionable and timeless. But she also pushed her own agenda as First Lady. She, for instance, sought to advocate for women's rights, LGBT rights, poverty awareness, education and healthy living. While largely refraining from involving herself at the sharp end of the most controversial political debates, she was nonetheless candid and straight-talking. David Axelrod (Obama's chief campaign strategist) was quoted in the *New Yorker* in 2008 as saying: 'Occasionally, it gives campaign people heartburn … She's fundamentally honest – goes out there, speaks her mind, jokes. She doesn't parse her words or select them with an antenna for political correctness.'

Through the vagaries of eight years in the White House, their marriage seemingly emerged as strong than ever. Speaking of her husband in 2012, she said: 'So when people ask me whether being in the White House has changed my husband, I can honestly say that when it comes to his character and his convictions and his heart, Barack Obama is still the same man I fell in love with all those years ago.' And he would tell *Vogue* in 2013: 'There's no doubt I'm a better man having spent time with Michelle,' adding that, 'I

THE VEGETABLE PATCH

Michelle Obama's efforts to counter childhood obesity included encouraging healthier eating. To give her campaign a spur, she planted a kitchen garden at the White House and established a bee colony. The White House thus provided organic fruit and vegetables, along with honey, to the First Family and to guests at state occasions. Echoing Eleanor Roosevelt's attempts to boost the American Second World War 'victory gardens' initiative by planting her own vegetable patch, Obama's efforts were indicative of the understated but effective way she went about being First Lady. 'My hope', she said, 'is that through children, they will begin to educate their families and that will, in turn, begin to educate our communities.'

would never say that Michelle's a better woman, but I will say she's a little more patient.' He perhaps best encapsulated her appeal to the wider public in a 2012 issue of *Ladies' Home Journal*:

The quality I love most about her is she's honest and genuine. I think that comes across to people. They get a sense that they can trust her. You know, the word 'authenticity' is overused these days. But I do think it captures what folks are looking for – not just in leaders, but also in friends and in co-workers – and that is, folks who are on the level. People like that tell you what they think and don't have a bunch of hidden motives. That's who Michelle is.

It is fair to say she played a vital role in defining the sort of president and, indeed, the sort of man Obama would become.

Parenthood
is the Top Job

'This is our first task – caring for our children.
It's our first job. If we don't get that right, we don't
get anything right. That's how, as a society,
we will be judged.'

BARACK OBAMA, 2012

Obama made the proclamation on the previous page at a vigil for the child victims of the Sandy Hook school shooting (see page 206). Amid a climate of grief and disbelief, the notion of protecting and nurturing society's youngest citizens had a particular resonance. For a man who spent eight years holding what is widely regarded as the most powerful job in the world, it is quite a statement to suggest that his role as a father is the more significant of the two posts. Yet, it is fair to believe that Obama was not merely issuing pleasantries but honestly holds that view. Introducing a fatherhood and mentoring initiative in 2010, he reflected:

> Over the course of my life, I have been an attorney, I've been a professor, I've been a state senator, I've been a US senator – and I currently am serving as president of the United States. But I can say without hesitation that the most challenging, most fulfilling, most important job I will have during my time on this Earth is to be Sasha and Malia's dad.

Obama's detachment from his own father – replete with psychological repercussions as he sought to define himself in the absence of a male role model – left him ruminating on the duties and responsibilities of a parent from a young age. As president, he emphasized again and again the importance of the paternal role and the need for fathers to step up to the mark. 'Fathers are our first teachers and coaches, mentors and role models,' he said on Father's Day in 2010. 'They push us to succeed, encourage us when we are struggling, and offer unconditional care and support.' The following year, in an article for *Parade*, he described the most fundamental duty of fathers as 'to show their children, by example, the kind of people they want them to become'. That he had been deprived of such an example, at least for any prolonged period, merely consolidated his view that the job of parenting is central to the well-being of both the individual child and society as a whole. As he put it in 2009: 'There's no rule that says you have to repeat your father's mistakes.'

That is not to say, however, that he does not acknowledge that parenting is sometimes a complex and difficult business. At that Sandy Hook vigil he spoke emotively on the subject: 'Someone once described the joy and anxiety of parenthood as the equivalent of having your heart outside of your body all the time, walking around.' But when he was faced with the prospect of becoming a parent himself, he embraced it wholeheartedly. Years later, when a journalist suggested in 2015 that the Supreme Court judgement in favour of same-sex marriage capped what represented his 'best week', he responded that his marriage to Michelle and the birth of his children were more likely contenders for the accolade.

Malia was the first to appear on the scene in 1998, with a sister, Sasha, coming along three years later. In January 2009, just prior to his inauguration, he published an open letter to his daughters in *Parade*. 'And suddenly, all my big plans for myself didn't seem so important anymore,' he wrote. 'I soon found that the greatest joy in my life was the joy I saw in yours. And I realized that my own life wouldn't count for much unless I was able to ensure that you had every opportunity for happiness and fulfillment in yours.'

Despite the significant demands upon their time made by their respective professional careers, the Obamas worked hard in tandem to give their daughters full and rewarding childhoods. There were the soccer matches, tennis training, dance and drama classes, and music lessons. As far as they could, the Obamas ran a regular family operation – of the type Barack had missed out on in his own younger days. When he won the presidency, he used his victory speech to reiterate a promise he had made to his daughters. They would be getting a puppy to keep them company in the White House – a bid to normalize an entirely abnormal situation for the young pair. Sure enough, a Portuguese Water Dog – a gift from Edward Kennedy, as it happened – was brought into the family unit. Bo even came to be known as the First Dog.

As the husband of a self-made woman and father of two

daughters, Obama has also been vociferous in arguing that girls everywhere should be encouraged to optimize their talents and chase their dreams. In the letter published in *Parade* he wrote of his wish for them and every other girl in the country 'to grow up in a world with no limits on your dreams and no achievements beyond your reach, and to grow into compassionate, committed women who will help build that world'. Later in the year, he sought to make the same argument at a speech in Cairo, in a region where large numbers of girls and women continue to be funnelled into traditional, domesticated roles. 'I am convinced that our daughters can contribute just as much to society as our sons,' he urged. 'Our common prosperity will be advanced by allowing all humanity, men and women, to reach their full potential.'

As they have got older, each daughter has slowly taken her place in the public sphere. In 2016, for example, they travelled with their mother to Liberia to support the Let Girls Learn Peace Initiative, meeting with Liberia's then president, Ellen Johnson Sirleaf – the first elected female head of state in Africa. While Sasha has continued her schooling, Malia took her place at Harvard University in 2017. Earlier in the year she had been on an internship at the Weinstein Company, shortly before Harvey Weinstein became the focus of sexual misconduct allegations – claims that must surely have hurt the Obamas en masse given their position on gender equality. They subsequently issued a statement expressing their 'disgust' at the crimes he is charged with committing. Nonetheless, it has been largely an assured first few steps into adulthood for Malia as she begins to slowly emerge from the significant shadow cast by her celebrated parents.

It may be assumed that Barack will continue to take an active role in their progress, especially now he is freed from the constraints of high office. Obama the family man emerges starkly in these words of his at the Sandy Hook Prayer Vigil in 2012:

There's only one thing we can be sure of, and that is the love that we have – for our children, for our families, for each other. The warmth of a small child's embrace – that is true. The memories we have of them, the joy that they bring, the wonder we see through their eyes, that fierce and boundless love we feel for them, a love that takes us out of ourselves, and binds us to something larger – we know that's what matters. We know we're always doing right when we're taking care of them, when we're teaching them well, when we're showing acts of kindness. We don't go wrong when we do that.

Words Matter …

'The truth is, actually, words do inspire.
Words do help people get involved …'

BARACK OBAMA, 2008

Obama made the observation on the previous page in a debate with Hillary Clinton as the two vied for the Democratic presidential candidacy. 'Don't discount that power,' he continued. 'Because when the American people are determined that something is going to happen, then it happens.'

Obama not only recognizes the power of words but also happens to be a master at using them – both in the written and spoken form. His books, *Dreams From My Father* and *The Audacity of Hope*, marked him out not only as a serious thinker and major public figure but also as a bona fide literary talent. At the same time, his 2004 'Audacity of Hope' address to the Democratic National Convention revealed him to be among the pre-eminent orators of his time. To his critics, his command of language is sometimes used as a weapon against him. He is, they suggest, too wordy, too clever for his own good – somehow removed from the experiences of real people. For millions of others, though, it is his grasp of the power of words – and perhaps most immediately, his ability to deliver a spellbinding speech – that raises him above the political crowd. Here is a man who not only has big ideas but can communicate them, too.

A WAY WITH WORDS

Obama rarely overburdens a speech with multiple ideas, preferring to take a central theme and hammer it home. He is a skilled manipulator of the pregnant pause and adopts a relaxed demeanour that sets the listener at ease. His speeches, even in moments of the highest political drama, have rarely been tense affairs. He is also adept at employing rhetorical devices – for instance, repeating key phrases and adopting the rule of three (linking three words or phrases of increasing power, as in 'Tonight, we gather to affirm the greatness of our nation, not because of the height of our skyscrapers, or the power of our military, or the size of our economy…').

Obama has always understood how to evoke feelings in his audience. In 2009 the American writer and academic, Jay Parini, wrote a piece for the *Guardian* responding to Obama's inauguration speech:

If, as Gerard Manley Hopkins once suggested, poetry is 'the common language heightened', then President

Obama (how I loved typing that phrase for the first time) became a poet in his speech. He made the language itself resonate; and he did so not by fancy writing or superficially elevated diction or self-conscious parallelism in the syntax. Anyone who rereads the speech closely will see that he used only the simplest of words: 'new', 'nation', 'now', 'generation', 'common', 'courage', 'world'. And he spoke these words in straightforward cadences that have already become familiar, drawing them out to exactly the right length.

There are plentiful examples from the Obama canon of speeches to prove the point. Consider, for instance, the elegance and emotive quality of the following passage from that inauguration speech:

On this day, we gather because we have chosen hope over fear, unity of purpose over conflict and discord. On this day, we come to proclaim an end to the petty grievances and false promises, the recriminations and worn-out dogmas that for far too long have strangled our politics. We remain a young nation. But in the words of Scripture, the time has come to set aside childish things. The time has come to reaffirm our enduring spirit; to choose our better history; to carry forward that precious gift, that noble idea passed on from generation to generation: the God-given promise that all are equal, all are free, and all deserve a chance to pursue their full measure of happiness.

Harry Reid, the former Senate Majority Leader, related a telling exchange with Obama in 2009. Reid told him a speech he had just given was 'phenomenal' and Obama responded: 'I have a gift, Harry.' As Reid would emphasize, Obama was not seeking to brag but merely making a statement of fact. It is sometimes said that he completes the triumvirate of the great presidential speakers alongside Lincoln and JFK. The power to move with one's words is a powerful weapon indeed.

THE MAN OF LETTERS

Had Obama chosen never to embark on a political career, there is a good chance he would have won sustained fame and fortune on the basis of his writing output alone. As it is, the outstanding success of both *Dreams From My Father: A Story of Race and Inheritance* (1995) and *The Audacity of Hope* (2006) mark him out as one of the most significant literary voices of his generation. Since 2001, these two titles alone have sold close to 5 million copies. There has also been a young adult version of *Dreams From My Father* as well as *Of Thee I Sing: A Letter To My Daughters*, both published while Obama was president. While in the White House it is estimated that Obama earned some US$15 million from book sales, and he even earned two Grammys for the audiobook versions of *Dreams* and *Audacity*. But the best may be yet to come. With more time on his hands now he is out of office and able to speak his mind more freely, the publishing world anticipates his next literary efforts with glee – so much so that Penguin Random House signed Barack and Michelle on a joint deal reportedly worth US$65 million.

... But Deeds Matter More

'The truth is, actually, words do inspire.
Words do help people get involved ...'

BARACK OBAMA, 2009

The claim that Obama is a man of only words rather than action is one significantly flawed. Nonetheless, it has been one of the principal challenges of his political career to convince the voting public that he would back his undoubted eloquence with concrete action – qualitatively and quantitatively shaping the future, not merely describing how it should look. In delivering his doctrine of active change – beginning with his anti-apartheid speech at Occidental in 1981 – he has provided some profound insights into his psyche.

On announcing his candidacy for the presidency, for example, he said of his work as a community organizer in Chicago (which paid the relatively paltry sum of US$13,000 per year) that he was motivated 'by a single, simple, powerful idea – that I might play a small part in building a better America'. Moreover, in that role, which he described as 'the best education I ever had', he learned 'that ordinary people can do extraordinary things when they're given an opportunity'. Obama was thus able to claim not merely aspirations to make a difference but could point to a CV that proved he had already started down that path.

Desire for change without the commitment to see the job through, he has suggested, is worthless. In May 2016 he made the point to students at Howard University, telling them: 'You have to go through life with more than just passion for change; you need a strategy. I'll repeat that. I want you to have passion, but you have to have a strategy. Not just awareness, but action. Not just hashtags, but votes.'

That he would act decisively as president was a key aspect of his 2008 electoral campaign, especially when set against what he implied would be the inaction of an administration led by his Republican rival, John McCain. At a speech shortly before the election, he said:

> John McCain says he's about change too and so I guess his whole angle is 'watch out, George Bush – except for economic policy, health care policy, tax policy, education policy, foreign policy and Karl Rove style politics [Rove was a senior adviser to George W. Bush] – we're really gonna shake things up in Washington.' That's not change. That's just calling the same thing something different. But you can put lipstick on a pig – it's still a pig. You can wrap an old fish in a piece of paper called change; it's still going to stink after eight years. We've had enough of the same old thing.

Obama's urge to act has long roots. He has credited his mother with instilling in him 'a sense of service and empathy that eventually led me to become a community organizer'. He also took inspiration from those giants of the civil rights movement, who 'with courage and clear purpose ... somehow managed to change the world'. When explaining why he decided to run for the presidency in 2008, he quoted a phrase that Martin Luther King had used: 'the fierce urgency of now' – the sense that the time has come to stand up with purpose and be counted. He expanded upon this notion at his speech marking the fiftieth anniversary of the Selma marches:

> What greater expression of faith in the American experiment than this; what greater form of patriotism is there than the belief that America is not yet finished, that we are strong enough to be self-critical, that each successive generation can look upon our imperfections and decide that it is in our power to remake this nation to more closely align with our highest ideals? ... It's the idea held by generations of citizens who believed that America is a constant work in progress; who believed that loving this country requires more than singing its praises or avoiding uncomfortable truths. It requires the occasional disruption, the willingness to speak out for what is right, to shake up the status quo. That's America.

Yet for all his idealism, Obama also encapsulates an attitude of pragmatism. Take, for instance, his inauguration address in 2009 when he proclaimed:

> The question we ask today is not whether our government is too big or too small, but whether

it works – whether it helps families find jobs at a decent wage, care they can afford, a retirement that is dignified. Where the answer is yes, we intend to move forward. Where the answer is no, programs will end.

Swept into office on a wave of optimism, he immediately began the process of managing expectations. He was not, his words suggested, on some ideological crusade but instead was intent on doing whatever was necessary to make government work better for the people. The state can be judged on no other basis, he seemed to suggest, than whether its actions yield the desired result. Obama was also acutely aware that economic conditions were such that there was even less wriggle room than normal to prop up failing government schemes.

His comments following the killing of Trayvon Martin in 2013 revealed another aspect of his pragmatism – an understanding that not every problem may be solved by legislation. Instead, there are times when the role of the government (and that of the president, as its most powerful representative) is to urge others to play their role in instigating deep-rooted social change. Hence his call to arms to stakeholders including those in the business, religious and celebrity communities:

I'm not naïve about the prospects of some grand, new federal program. I'm not sure that that's what we're talking about here. But I do recognize that as president, I've got some convening power, and there are a lot of good programs that are being done across the country on this front. And for us to be able to gather together business leaders and local elected officials and clergy and celebrities and athletes, and figure out how are we doing a better job helping young African-American men feel that they're a full part of this society and that they've got pathways and avenues to succeed – I think that would be a pretty good outcome from what was obviously a tragic situation.

Moreover, he has sought to instil his own will for change into the generations coming up. In a speech to students at Illinois' Northwestern University in 2006, he warned against complacently falling into a life driven by self-interest. 'Focusing your life solely on making a buck shows a poverty of ambition,' he admonished. 'It asks too little of yourself. And it will leave you unfulfilled.' Three years later he told the students of Notre Dame University that carving out a better future lay squarely with them (especially in light of the economic crisis then engulfing much of the world). 'This generation, your generation is the one that must find a path back to prosperity,' he told them, adding that it was down to them to decide how to respond to a global economy 'where greed and short-term thinking were too often rewarded at the expense of fairness and diligence and an honest day's work'.

To act, he suggested, is a duty, and failure to act renders you impotent in the face of injustice or even mere circumstance. Yet rather than characterize this duty as an onerous burden,

Obama has more often discussed it in terms of a task to undertake with pride and passion – the act of participating to improve society also being a reflection of the individual's strength of character. Speaking on the fiftieth anniversary of the Selma marches in 2015, he gave this inspiring resumé of the nation's tradition of action:

> Look at our history. We're the immigrants who stowed away on ships to reach these shores, the huddled masses yearning to breathe free – Holocaust survivors, Soviet defectors, the Lost Boys of Sudan. We're the hopeful strivers who cross the Rio Grande because we want our kids to know a better life. That's how we came to be.
>
> We're the slaves who built the White House and the economy of the South. We're the ranch hands and cowboys who opened up the West, and countless laborers who laid rail, and raised skyscrapers, and organized for workers' rights.
>
> We're the fresh-faced GIs who fought to liberate a continent. And we're the Tuskeegee Airmen, and the Navajo code-talkers, and the Japanese Americans who fought for this country even as their own liberty had been denied.
>
> We're the firefighters who rushed into those buildings on 9/11, the volunteers who signed up to fight in Afghanistan and Iraq. We're the gay Americans whose blood ran in the streets of San Francisco and New York, just as blood ran down this bridge.

We are storytellers, writers, poets, artists who abhor unfairness, and despise hypocrisy, and give voice to the voiceless, and tell truths that need to be told.

... We are the people Langston Hughes wrote of who 'build our temples for tomorrow, strong as we know how'.

Obama's Heroes

'She was one of those quiet heroes that we have all across America. They're not famous. Their names are not in the newspapers, but each and every day they work hard … All they try to do is just do the right thing.'

BARACK OBAMA ON THE DEATH OF HIS GRANDMOTHER, MADELYN DUNHAM, 2008

To some, Obama is a hero in his own right. As a revered global figure – and it is true that his stock abroad has often been significantly higher than in his own country – he has achieved a stature that has arguably been unrivalled since the death of Nelson Mandela.

In fact, Mandela was identified by Obama in 2013 as 'a giant of history, who moved a nation toward justice, and in the process moved billions around the world'. The South African's influence on Obama was further reflected in 2017 when the former president tweeted these words of Mandela:

> No one is born hating another person because of the colour of his skin or his background or his religion … People must learn to hate, and if they can learn to hate, they can be taught to love … For love comes more naturally to the human heart than its opposite.

Tweeted in the immediate aftermath of violence at an anti-racism protest in Charlottesville, Virginia, it quickly broke the record for most 'likes' for a single tweet and confirmed the enduring influence of both men. But which other towering figures have inspired Obama over the years?

It is notable that Obama has emphasized that heroes need not, in fact, be 'towering figures' at all. As the quotation at the start of this section shows, he sees perhaps greater value in the 'quiet heroes', ordinary men and women striving to do the right – and sometimes extraordinary – things. The idea of looking close to home for one's heroes was a notion he also explored in remarks he made on Father's Day in 2008, describing the importance of fathers as 'teachers and coaches ... mentors and role models'. A year later, he was again elevating the 'quiet hero'. Scientists and engineers, he said, 'ought to stand side by side with athletes and entertainers as role models'.

However, that is not to say that Obama has no room for the famous among his own pantheon of heroic figures. He has, for instance, cited several of his presidential predecessors as particularly worthy of praise – among them, Thomas Jefferson and Andrew Jackson, Franklin Roosevelt and John F. Kennedy. But it is perhaps Abraham Lincoln who stands pre-eminent among them in Obama's opinion. He was not, Obama has acknowledged, without flaws but his willingness to do what was necessary to effect real change chimes strongly with Obama's own view of how the presidential office should operate. In 2011 he said:

I think it's fair to say that Abraham Lincoln had convictions. But he constantly was making concessions and compromises. I've got the Emancipation Proclamation hanging up in the Oval Office, and if you read that document – for those of you who have not read it – it doesn't emancipate everybody. It actually declares the slaves who are in areas that have rebelled against the Union are free but it carves out various provinces, various parts of various states, that are still in the Union, [where] you can keep your slaves. Now, think about that. 'The Great Emancipator' was making a compromise in the Emancipation Proclamation because he thought it was necessary in terms of advancing the goals of preserving the Union and winning the war. And then, ultimately, after the war was completed, you then had the thirteenth and fourteenth and fifteenth amendments [related to the abolition of slavery, and the citizenship and voting rights of African Americans].

And what about those from beyond America's borders? In 2009, the president responded to a question about who, dead or alive, he would most like to dine with by nominating the Indian independence leader, Mahatma Gandhi. 'He's somebody who I find a lot of inspiration in,' he explained. 'He inspired Dr King, so if it hadn't been for the non-violent movement in India, you might not have seen the same non-violent movement for civil rights here in the United States.' He also showed his admiration for Cesar Chavez (1927–93), the famed Latino American labour leader and civil rights activist, whom Obama described as 'one of America's greatest champions for social justice', when he suggested he was another whose tactics could be traced back to Gandhi.

Predictably, the black civil rights movement of the 1960s throws up a host of figures who have inspired Obama, not only for shaking off the shackles of race discrimination but because they epitomize a desire to effect change through extraordinary organizational abilities. The civil rights movement proved that when people come together – even those who are oppressed and downtrodden – they can make a difference. That has been a message that Obama has carried with him throughout his political life.

As the single most important figure in the black civil rights movement, King holds a particular place in his heart. Speaking on the occasion of the federal holiday to mark King's birthday in 2015, Obama spoke of him as a:

… champion for justice [who] helped awaken our nation's long-slumbering conscience and inspired a generation. Through a cacophony of division and hatred, his voice rang out, challenging America to make freedom a reality for all of God's children and prophesying a day when the discord of our Union would be transformed into a symphony of brotherhood. His clarion call echoed the promise of our founding – that each of us are created equal – and every day he worked to give meaning to this timeless creed.

But Obama has also been careful to give space to other prominent figures in the movement, aware that King would not have recorded such achievements without their efforts too. In his speech to mark the fiftieth anniversary of the Selma marches of 1965, he gave a roll call of some of the most important:

- Ralph Abernathy (1926–90). A church minister and close confidant of King, Abernathy co-founded the influential Southern Christian Leadership Conference (SCLC) with him. He was integral to such actions as the Montgomery bus boycott in the 1950s that followed the arrest of Rosa Parks for refusing to relinquish her seat to a white passenger. He was president of the SCLC between King and Joseph Lowery (see below).
- Amelia Boynton (1911–2015). A civil rights activist particularly famed for her pivotal involvement in the Selma marches of 1965 (see page 58).
- Fannie Lou Hamer (1917–77). A leading campaigner for voting rights and women's rights, most prominently in Mississippi. She co-founded the National Women's Political Caucus, which aimed to identify and support women from all racial backgrounds who sought to hold public office.
- John Lewis (1940–). One of the organizers of the 1963 march on Washington, which culminated with King's 'I have a dream' speech. Lewis has subsequently served in the US House of Representatives for Georgia's 5th congressional district.
- Joseph Lowery (1921–). A Methodist minister who helped organize the Montgomery bus boycott. He co-founded

the SCLC and ultimately succeeded King, following after Abernathy, as its president.

- Diane Nash (1938–). She undertook several notable campaigns including protests demanding desegregated lunch counters and interstate travel. She also established a number of voting rights initiatives that helped pave the way for the Voting Rights Act of 1965.

- Fred Shuttlesworth (1922–2011). A minister in Birmingham, Alabama, and co-founder of the SCLC. He was a key figure in the 1963 Birmingham Campaign to highlight the city's racial divisions. King would describe Birmingham as the most segregated city in the country.

- C. T. Vivian (1924–). Another church minister and member of the King inner circle. King is said to have described him as 'the greatest preacher to ever live'.

- Hosea Williams (1926–2000). One of King's inner circle within the SCLC, Williams was key to organizing numerous mass actions. King referred to him as his 'bull in a china closet'.

- Andrew Young (1932–). A pastor-cum-activist, he served as executive director of the SCLC. In later years he held various political offices, including as a US Congressman from Georgia, US Ambassador to the UN, and as mayor of Atlanta.

Obama has also spoken in praise of Jackie Robinson (1919–72), the first African American to play Major League baseball, when the Booklyn Dodgers broke the colour line to sign him in 1947. Robinson joined the Baseball Hall of Fame in 1962.

Obama has additionally reserved special acclaim for a number of inspirational women from throughout American history. Among them:

- Sacajawea, the celebrated Shoshone Indian interpreter who assisted the Lewis and Clark Expedition that mapped and explored the western part of the United States in the first decade of the nineteenth century.
- Sojourner Truth (born Isabella Baumfree), a former slave who campaigned for abolition and women's rights.
- Susan B. Anthony, one of the leading suffragists in the early part of the twentieth century.

THE KENNEDYS

Obama has sometimes been regarded as a spiritual descendent of the Kennedy dynasty, nor has he been reticent in admitting his admiration for them. In describing JFK in 2011, he might even have been talking about himself:

John F. Kennedy chose a life in the arena, full of confidence that our country could surmount any obstacle, as he'd seen it do himself. He chose a life of leadership, fired not by naïve optimism, but committed realism; 'idealism', as his wife Jackie put it, 'without illusions'.

Bobby, meanwhile, had 'charisma and eloquence – that unique ability, rare for most but common among Kennedys, to sum up the hopes and dreams of the most diverse nation on Earth with a simple phrase or sentence; to inspire even the most apathetic observers of American life'. He believed, Obama said in 2005, that America is a 'place where we're not afraid to face down the greatest challenges in pursuit of the greater good; a place where, against all odds, we overcome'. Arguably Bobby's most well-known utterance was a paraphrasing of George Bernard Shaw: 'There are those that look at things the way they are, and ask why? I dream of things that never were, and ask why not?' It is a belief very close to Obama's own guiding principles. But while Obama was too young to ever know John or Bobby, their younger brother Ted became a trusted and valued colleague. In particular, Obama admired his many thwarted attempts to introduce healthcare reform – a cause that was a vital component of Obama's presidential programme. As such, he regarded Ted as 'the greatest legislator of our time'.

Read Like Obama

'Reading is important. If you know how to read,
then the whole world opens up to you.'

BARACK OBAMA, 2013

Obama is known as a prodigious reader, consuming texts across all sorts of genres, from great novels to political biographies and philosophical treatises. Moreover, he has been a staunch public advocate for the power of reading, regularly sharing his personal recommendations through the mainstream media, social media and personal interactions. In an interview with Marilynne Robinson for the *New York Review of Books* in 2015, he outlined how instrumental he believes his consumption of literature has been to his personal development:

> When I think about how I understand my role as citizen, setting aside being president, and the most important set of understandings that I bring to that position of citizen, the most important stuff I've learned I think I've learned from novels. It has to do with empathy. It has to do with being comfortable with the notion that the world is complicated and full of grays, but there's still truth there to be found, and that you have to strive for that and work for that. And

the notion that it's possible to connect with some[one] else even though they're very different from you.

Given the number of Obama's literary recommendations, it has been possible to put together an extensive list of texts he has read and loved over the years. For a man who has repeatedly avowed strong Christian convictions, it is unsurprising that the Bible ranks high among his list of all-time best reads. He is also known to have a penchant for some of the classics of English literature. Shakespeare (the tragedies in particular), F. Scott Fitzgerald, Graham Greene, Herman Melville, Robert Louis Stevenson and John Steinbeck are all known to have featured on his reading syllabus, as has the Saint Lucian poet (and winner of the 1992 Nobel Prize for Literature) Derek Walcott. Appealing to his spirit of adventure are children's classics including Edward Stratemeyer's *Hardy Boys* series and the Harry Potter novels of J. K. Rowling.

At the same time, Obama is steeped in knowledge of his predecessors in the White House, having read, for instance, the collected writings of Abraham Lincoln, and Doris Kearns Goodwin's analysis of his presidency, *Team of Rivals*. Indeed, he even summoned Goodwin to the Oval Office for a discussion about her book. David McCullough's well-regarded biography of the US's second president, John Adams, is another to have lain on the Obama bedside table, as has *The Rise of Theodore Roosevelt* by Edmund Morris and several works on the presidency of Franklin Delano Roosevelt (among them *Defining Moment: FDR's*

Hundred Days and the Triumph of Hope by Jonathan Alte and *FDR* by Jean Edward Smith). The high esteem in which Obama holds Martin Luther King Jr is also reflected in his attachment to Taylor Branch's epic biographical trilogy of the civil rights leader's life and times. But arguably the autobiography he has found most instructive is *The Story of My Experiments with Truth*, consisting of the writings of the chief architect of India's independence from the United Kingdom, Mahatma Gandhi.

In terms of political philosophy, Obama has praised Adam Smith's *Theory of Moral Sentiments*, an eighteenth-century work that laid out Smith's general philosophical position ahead of publication of *The Wealth of Nations* – often considered to be the founding text of modern economics. From the same century, he has studied Alexander Hamilton, James Madison and John Jay's *Federalist Papers* (a series of essays written under the pseudonym of 'Publius' with the aim of promoting the ratification of the US Constitution). Ralph Waldo Emerson's 1841 essay, 'Self-Reliance', impacted him with its call for individual truth over mindless conformity. And among twentieth-century thinkers, Obama is a known admirer of Reinhold Niebuhr – who wrote extensively on issues of politics, government and religion in works such as *The Nature and Destiny of Man* – and W. E. B. Du Bois, whose 1903 collection of essays entitled *Souls of Black Folk* reframed the debate over race relations in the US.

While Aleksandr Solzhenitsyn gave Obama insight into the dark side of the Soviet state, *Best and the Brightest* (David

Read Like Obama

Halberstam) and *Lessons in Disaster* (Gordon Goldstein) returned the focus to America, and its involvement in Vietnam in particular. Studs Terkel's *Working* provides a snapshot of attitudes to work in American society, while Ralph Ellison's classic 1952 novel, *Invisible Man*, explores some of the key questions and challenges that faced African Americans in the twentieth century. Politically themed works he has read of more recent vintage include Thomas L. Fiedman's *Hot, Flat and Crowded: Why We Need a Green Revolution,* Jeffrey Sachs' *Common Wealth: Economics for a Crowded Planet,* Steve Coll's *Ghost Wars: The Secret History of the CIA, Afghanistan, and Bin Laden* and Larry Bartels' *Unequal Democracy: The Political Economy of the New Gilded Age.* Another title on Obama's reading roster, *All the King's Men* by Robert Penn Warren, tells the tale of the rise of a populist politician called Willie Stark – a story with doubtless added resonance in the Trump era.

Obama is also well engaged with contemporary fiction, despite the many other claims upon his time. He has praised the work of Nobel Laureate Toni Morrison, for instance, as well as the novels of Marilynne Robinson, his *New York Times Review of Books* interviewer. Other genres to have won his readership include the hard-edged science fiction of Liu Cixin, the magic realism of Salman Rushdie, the American panoramic of Kent Haruf, the urban grit of Richard Prince and the lyricism of Lauren Goff.

Increasing the rate of American literacy was a key tenet of Obama's education policy while in office. In 2005 he told the Annual Conference of the American Library

Association that 'we all have responsibilities as parents, as librarians, as educators, as politicians, and as citizens to instill in our children a love of reading so that we can give them a chance to fulfill their dreams'. Rarely has an American president worn his love of literature so openly on his sleeve.

Keep the Big Picture in Focus

'This [Democratic] party … has always made the biggest difference in the lives of the American people when we led, not by polls, but by principle; not by calculation, but by conviction; when we summoned the entire nation to a common purpose – a higher purpose.'

BARACK OBAMA, 2007

High-level politics with its dark arts has a knack of challenging even the most ethical figure to stick by their principles. For many, the demands of juggling competing interests while maintaining a grasp on power are too much, and their original, well-intentioned aims give way to realpolitik. As we shall see, Obama was never afraid of the compromise if it heightened the chances of progressing his broader aims. There were times, too, when he undoubtedly became bogged down in the nitty-gritty of confrontational politics. Yet even in the toughest times he showed a remarkable resilience and ability to keep in sight his 'first principles'.

He laid out the fundamental terms of his political manifesto no more clearly than in his remarks to the UN General Assembly in September 2016: 'I believe in a liberal political order – an order built not just through elections and representative government, but also through respect for human rights and civil society, and independent judiciaries and the rule of law.'

At the first presidential debate with Mitt Romney in 2012, he went into a little more detail as to how he views the role of government:

The first role of the federal government is to keep the American people safe. That's its most basic function … But I also believe that the federal government has the capacity to help open up opportunity and create ladders of opportunity and to create frameworks where the American people can succeed. As Abraham Lincoln understood, there are also some things we do better together. So, in the middle of the Civil War, Abraham Lincoln said, let's help to finance the Transcontinental Railroad, let's start land grant colleges, because we want to give these gateways of opportunity for all Americans, because if all Americans are getting opportunity, we're all going to be better off. That doesn't restrict people's freedom. That enhances it. What I've tried to do as president is to apply those same principles.

Defence of the people and the creation of opportunities for all – or, to put it another way, nurturing the American dream – were thus the anchoring tenets of his time in office. How successful he was in achieving these aims is for history to judge, but it is easy to track their consistent influence on him during his presidency.

At the 2017 opening of the first Obama Foundation Summit, he gave an insight into an even more fundamental set of axioms that he has striven to follow. These were, as he explained, 'values that my mother had whispered in my ear' and included:

- Be kind and be useful and caring about people who are less fortunate than you
- Be a peacemaker rather than an instigator
- Try to lift people up instead of putting them down

The idea of public office as being to put oneself in the service of others was thus a concept that had been long ingrained in him. As he put it to the Democratic National Convention in 2012: 'a freedom without a commitment to others, a freedom without love or charity or duty or patriotism, is unworthy of our founding ideals'. As for his own 'founding ideals', he neatly outlined them again in his 2009 inaugural address:

Our challenges may be new. The instruments with which we meet them may be new. But those values upon which our success depends – honesty and hard work, courage and fair play, tolerance and curiosity, loyalty and patriotism – these things are old. These things are true. They have been the quiet force of progress throughout our history. What is demanded then is a return to these truths. What is required of us now is a new era of responsibility – a recognition, on the part of every American, that we have duties to ourselves, our nation, and the world, duties that we do not grudgingly accept but rather seize gladly, firm in the knowledge that there is nothing so satisfying to the spirit, so defining of our character, than giving our all to a difficult task.

Obstacles are There to be Overcome

'But always remember that, no matter what obstacles stand in our way, nothing can stand in the way of the power of millions of voices calling for change.'

BARACK OBAMA, 2008

As he has liked to point out, Obama's story has been an unlikely one. At turn after turn he has faced seemingly insurmountable odds yet managed to overcome them. A kid of mixed heritage with an African name becoming president of the United States? Ridiculous. Except, of course, he proved that it wasn't.

The process of overturning the odds started early. One might, for instance, point to the manner in which the confused and troubled teen in search of a father figure turned things around to earn a place first at Columbia and then Harvard. Then he confounded expectations to become the first black president of the *Harvard Law Review* and subsequently earned accolades as author of one of the most notable memoirs of recent times (in 2016 the *Guardian* ranked *Dreams From My Father* number five in the list of the 100 greatest works of non-fiction). And all of that before his political career had even started in earnest.

After several years in Chicago working in academia and as a civil rights attorney, Obama undertook his first campaign for public office in 1995 when he ran for the Illinois State Senate. He won a seat but it was not without considerable personal cost. His mother, who had been suffering from cancer, had returned to Hawaii while Obama stayed in Chicago to fight the election. As a result, he was not with her when she died – something he puts among the greatest regrets of his life. Taking up his seat also meant spending a large part of the week in the state capital, Springfield, and away from, first, Michelle and then, in later years, from his young growing family in Chicago. Nonetheless, he took it all on the chin and threw himself into the maelstrom of state politics. Among his achievements were reforms to the provision of after-school programmes, funding for housing improvements and an overhaul of political funding in the state.

Having come a long way in quick time, he soon fixed his attentions on his next goal – a move up the political ladder. After considering and then dismissing the idea of running for mayor of Chicago, he opted instead to try to win a seat in the House of Representatives. At the election in 2000 he challenged the popular incumbent, veteran civil rights activist Bobby Rush. His campaign took a hit when he was widely criticized for missing a vote on gun control legislation in the State Senate because he was in Hawaii, visiting a sick Malia. Losing the election by some thirty percentage points, Obama admitted that he had 'my rear end handed to me' but he characteristically used the experience to his advantage. According to Toni Periwinkle, a member of the Chicago City Council and an early Obama ally, he 'took a hard look at himself after that campaign and became a much better campaigner, more at ease on the campaign trail'. Obama also appointed David Axelrod as a skilled campaign strategist and refocused his immediate efforts on his work in the Illinois Senate – a tactic that saw him re-elected to his seat unopposed in 2002. Even after hitting a hurdle hard, Obama had managed to regain his stride.

Moreover, in 2002 he stuck his head above the parapet to speak out against the US-led invasion of Iraq, which President George W. Bush had enthusiastically championed. Coming shortly on the heels of the devastating 9/11 terrorist attacks of 2001, it took a brave soul to suggest America was immersing itself in an ill-starred venture – even more so when your middle name is Hussein and your surname rhymes with Osama. But in a powerful piece of oration, Obama condemned the conflict as 'a dumb war … a rash war. What I am opposed to is the cynical attempt by Richard Perle and Paul Wolfowitz [central figures in the Bush administration] and other armchair, weekend warriors in this administration to shove their own ideological agendas down our throats, irrespective of the costs in lives lost and in hardships borne.' Years later, the speech would galvanize Obama's support as he sought to beat Hillary Clinton for the Democratic nomination, since Clinton had not voted against the war. By 2008, opposition was widespread to what had become a difficult and unpopular war but back in 2002 it represented a huge risk for a little-known state politician looking to step up.

Obstacles are There to be Overcome

Two years later, Obama announced his intention to run for one of Illinois' two seats in the US Senate. Again, he faced an uphill task. There were very few senators as young as him (he was still in his early forties) and in 125 years there had been only four African Americans elected to the Senate. As he commented on the campaign trail: 'There are some who might say that somebody named Barack Obama can't be elected senator in the state of Illinois.' But having quickly honed his campaign skills in the light of lessons learned from his experience in 2000, he was soon favourite to win. Then came his great breakthrough. Selected to give the keynote speech at the Democratic National Convention, Obama delivered one of the great political addresses of recent decades – his 'Audacity of Hope' oration with its message of unity and renewal. It thrust him into the front line of national political life and is likely to remain a model of speech-making for years to come. Sure enough, in November 2004 he was elected comfortably to the Senate – a victory that prompted his resignation from the State Senate.

As a senator he concentrated on several areas of particular interest, including housing, schools and healthcare. However, it was also a time of frustration as he began to familiarize himself with the obstructive nature of Washington politics. He had come to the national capital to get things done, but it was not always that easy. As he jokingly told the Gridiron Club in 2006: 'I've been very blessed. Keynote speaker at the Democratic convention. The cover of *Newsweek*. My book made the best-seller list. I just won a Grammy for reading it on tape. Really, what else is there to do? Well, I guess I could pass a law or something.'

Still his ambition burned to get himself even closer to the centre of power, even if logic suggested he was propelling himself towards ever larger obstacles. That was, though, to underestimate his determination. 'Making your mark on the world is hard,' he said in a speech in Washington in 2006. 'If it were easy, everybody would do it. But it's not. It takes patience, it takes commitment, and it comes with plenty of failure along the way. The real test is not whether you avoid this failure, because you won't. It's whether you let it harden or shame you into inaction, or whether you learn from it; whether you choose to persevere.'

Come 2007 and, against the advice of many of those close to him, Obama announced his intention to run for the White House. Later that year he would tell the Democratic National Committee: 'I never expected to be here, I always knew this journey was improbable. I've never been on a journey that wasn't.' The notion of doing that which others tell you is impossible became a central plank of his presidential campaign. Picking up on a slogan first used in 2006 by Massachusetts Governor Deval Patrick, Obama adopted the rallying cry of 'Yes, we can.' Speaking on the day of the New Hampshire Primary in 2008, he said, 'For when we have faced down impossible odds, when we've been told we're not ready or that we shouldn't try or that we can't, generations of Americans have responded with a simple creed that sums up the spirit of a people: Yes, we can.' And millions of people began to believe him.

He was reiterating a point he had made the previous year at an address at the University of Iowa. On that occasion, he had said: 'Never forget that we have it within our power to shape history in this country. It is not in our character to sit idly by as victims of fate or circumstance, for we are a people of action and innovation, forever pushing the boundaries of what's possible.' Even as he celebrated his victory in the presidential election in November 2008, he was aware that the path ahead remained precarious. At a rally in Chicago's Grant Park, he told the elated crowds: 'The road ahead will be long. Our climb will be steep. We may not get there in one year or even in one term. But, America, I have never been more hopeful than I am tonight that we will get there.'

The ultimate overturner of odds and conqueror of obstacles, Obama seems almost to be energized when facing problems and challenges – some circumstantial in nature, others thrust into his way by opponents. He is a man who thrives in the presence of impediments. Consider, for instance, his joyous contrariness when he told *The New York Times Magazine* in 2010: 'There is probably a perverse pride in my administration … that we were going to do the right thing, even if short-term it was unpopular.'

Social Networks are Political Networks

'Were it not for the internet, Barack Obama would not be president. Were it not for the internet, Barack Obama would not have been the nominee.'

SARIANNA HUFFINGTON, NOVEMBER 2008

Obama is widely regarded as the first global political figure to really 'get' social media. At a time when many of his older, more experienced opponents struggled even to know what Facebook or Twitter were, Obama – a self-confessed 'nerd' – was embracing them to spread his political message and raise his profile. Given that social media has been a playground predominantly for the young, he was able to tap into a vast swathe of the population who, voting patterns suggested, had become bored by the political world. By engaging with young, liberally inclined and racially diverse users of social networks, he not only garnered votes that might otherwise have eluded him (and, in many cases, any candidate) but was also able to mobilize an army of supporters who spread the word among their real-world social circles, too. Nor should the role of social networking in his fundraising efforts be overlooked.

Obama has not been shy to acknowledge the importance of the internet in his career. 'I think part of the reason that I have been successful,' he told *Business Insider* in September 2016, '… is there is this whole other media ecology out there of the internet and Instagram and memes and talk shows and comedy, and I'm pretty good at that.'

Indeed, he is. In 2007, Obama's route to the White House seemed treacherous. Firstly, he had to overcome the red-hot favourite for the Democratic nomination, Hillary Clinton – a former First Lady who had proven her own political mettle as the Governor of New York. Sure, there were plenty of people who loathed the Clintons, but Hillary was nonetheless regarded as a bastion of the political firmament. Most political commentators were wondering if America was ready for its first female president – not its first African-American one.

Undeterred, Obama reached out to the movers and shakers of Silicon Valley in a bid to discover how the internet and new media might help his campaign. Where Thomas Jefferson had recognized the power of the newspapers, Franklin Delano Roosevelt the radio and John F. Kennedy the television, Obama similarly sought to understand how the emerging media forms of the age could be put to work in his interests. By the summer of 2008 he had upset the odds so that Clinton withdrew from the race for the Democratic nomination. Now he faced the Republican, John McCain – a bona fide war hero, no less – in the battle for the Oval Office. Sensationally, Obama rode a wave of optimism to win by 200 electoral college votes and some 8.5 million popular votes.

People termed it the 'Facebook election', which was doubtless an oversimplification but, nonetheless, the raw data was telling. Obama managed to secure some 5 million 'friends' across assorted social media campaigns, 3 million of them on Facebook. In comparison, McCain could claim just 600,000 Facebook friends (and during the race for the Democratic nomination, Clinton had garnered just over 3,000 by the time Obama had notched up a quarter of a million). On Twitter, meanwhile, Obama had 115,000 followers while McCain had just 5,000. At a moment when the Kardashians were only just entering the public consciousness, these were seriously impressive figures. YouTube proved even more fertile, with some 50 million people watching an aggregate 14 million hours of videos uploaded by the Obama camp (the McCain figures were about a quarter of his rival's). Will.i.am's 'Yes We Can' video clip went spectacularly viral, receiving millions of views within days. Then there were the 13 million people on the Obama email list, who together received 7,000 variations of over 1 billion emails (with 3 million more receiving text messages between five and twenty times per month).

For relatively little outlay (social media campaigns are, per capita, much cheaper than, say, a prime-time TV ad campaign), Obama secured the vast majority of the young vote. More than that, though, he built a movement. And then he did it all over again in 2012.

This time facing Mitt Romney, his numbers were once more formidable – 21 million Twitter followers to Romney's 1.5 million, 31 million Facebook friends to Romney's 10.5 million, and 250 million video views to Romney's 30 million. A second term beckoned.

Of course, social media can be a source of harm as well

WHERE THE MONEY'S AT

Social media was also crucial to funding the
Obama campaign, especially after he became the
first major-party presidential candidate in decades
to turn down public financing (if he had accepted
it, his opportunity to privately fundraise would have
been seriously curtailed under electoral regulations).
Around 6.5 million online donations netted him
over US$500 million in campaign funding – with
twelve in every thirteen donations being for
less than US$100. Candidates have traditionally
relied on a few huge donations to bankroll their
electoral campaigns, but Obama had used the new
technology to overturn this model at a stroke.

---

as good, and Obama has recognized the risks. Speaking at
a Town Hall meeting in 2010, for example, he noted: 'The
internet and Twitter and all these things are very powerful,
but it also means sometimes that instead of having a
dialogue we just start calling ... each other names. And
that's true on the left or the right.' By the end of his
tenure, there were growing concerns about the volume of
disinformation on the internet, and its potential to skew
democracy. By the time Donald Trump had brought the
phrase 'fake news' into common parlance, Obama told a

news conference in Berlin in November 2016: 'If we are not serious about facts and what's true and what's not … if we can't discriminate between serious arguments and propaganda, then we have problems.'

While it is painfully evident that social media is a creature that cannot be tamed by any single individual, Obama nonetheless managed to harness its energy in an extraordinary and unprecedented fashion. In 2008 Joe Trippi, a Democratic strategist and political consultant, said of the new man in the White House: 'Just like Kennedy brought in the television presidency, I think we're about to see the first wired, connected, networked presidency.' Few could argue that his prediction did not come to pass.

AMERICA'S FIRST AFRICAN-AMERICAN PRESIDENT

The build-up to the 2008 US presidential election was extraordinary in that the two major challengers for the Democratic candidacy were Obama and Hillary Clinton – a black man and a woman, demographic groups that had never previously provided a US president. For much of the world, Obama's eventual victory came out of nowhere and it marked a sea change in the American political landscape that can be traced back to the Civil Rights Act and Voting Rights Act of the 1960s – two pieces of legislation that opened the path for African-American candidates. In 1972 Shirley Chisholm became the first black candidate for the presidential nomination of a major party – the Democrats – although she fought in primaries only across a few states. Then in the 1980s Jesse Jackson fought for the Democratic nomination, running in primaries nationwide and garnering some 7 million popular votes in his second campaign in 1988. It was only in the 1990s that the Republicans fielded an African-American candidate in presidential primaries. Into the twenty-first century, Colin Powell and Condoleezza Rice both served as Secretary of State (in the administration of George W. Bush) – the most senior government positions hitherto occupied by African Americans. But still the presidency itself seemed a way off – until Obama.

Set the Agenda

'There is not a liberal America and a conservative America – there is the United States of America. There is not a Black America and a White America and Latino America and Asian America – there's the United States of America.'

BARACK OBAMA, ADDRESS TO THE NATIONAL DEMOCRATIC CONVENTION, 2004

One of Obama's great attributes is his ability to get to grips with complex arguments. As a result, he has consistently been able to lay out a clear vision of how he intends to act in any given situation. Where his opponents attempt to set the agenda, he has had the knack of wrestling it from them. An ability to communicate his assessment of the biggest problems to be faced and how they may be dealt with not only ensured that the electorate felt safe in his hands but that many millions of voters were positively energized by his world view.

The quotation at the beginning of this section, from his famous Democratic Convention speech in 2004, is a good example of his agenda-setting skills. With the nation then still psychologically reeling from the 9/11 attacks and immersed in, it was becoming apparent, difficult conflicts in Afghanistan and Iraq, Obama sensed the public mood. He recognized the divisions that had become exacerbated during the Bush years – between ethnic and religious groups, but also between those desperate for more rapid social change and those who already felt that change was moving too fast. With statements such as the one above,

Set the Agenda

Obama seized the initiative where more experienced politicians had found no way to do so. He evoked an America not divided but unified, one rooted in a history of immigration. A nation essentially optimistic, hard-working and full of initiative. Of course, not everyone was convinced but many were and alerted others to the words of this political upstart. Obama-ism as a mass movement was born.

While remaining bound to his core messages of hope and change in his run for the White House in 2007 and 2008, he also continued to agenda-set. Where the 'Audacity of Hope' oration had given the world a taste of his big-picture vision, he knew he needed to communicate specifics, too. For example, in his speech at the New Hampshire Primary in early 2008, he spoke of 'the common threats of the twenty-first century' that he would seek to address as president: 'terrorism and nuclear weapons, climate change and poverty, genocide and disease'. He also talked of breaking the 'tyranny of oil', which many in the country had come to feel was behind the US's rush to war with Iraq. On the campaign trail, Obama would repeat his foreign policy priorities: the anti-terrorism fight, the ending of the wars in Afghanistan and Iraq, moves towards reducing the threat from nuclear weapons and a promise to close the controversial detention centre at Guantanamo Bay (see page 187). These were real policy goals to which ordinary voters could relate.

He was similarly transparent in his domestic aims. There is too much economic inequality, he argued, which is stifling progress and restricting equality of opportunity.

Regulation of the financial sector was on the cards, as well as efforts to boost the industrial and manufacturing sectors. Education, housing and energy were also squarely within his sights. His other great domestic 'headline-grabber' was his plan to overhaul healthcare insurance – a long-term aim of many in the Democratic ranks but a subject guaranteed to divide American opinion. Controversial or not, his agenda was clear and voters had a real sense of what they were getting.

Having won the election, he again laid out his policy priorities in his inauguration address, as when he noted:

> That we are in the midst of crisis is now well understood. Our nation is at war, against a far-reaching network of violence and hatred. Our economy is badly weakened, a consequence of greed and irresponsibility on the part of some, but also our collective failure to make hard choices and prepare the nation for a new age. Homes have been lost; jobs shed; businesses shuttered. Our health care is too costly; our schools fail too many; and each day brings further evidence that the ways we use energy strengthen our adversaries and threaten our planet.

Despite sharing the same vision on many issues, the contest for the Democratic nomination between Obama and Clinton had been brutal. At the height of the battle in early 2008, for instance, she had said of him: 'There's a big difference between us – speeches versus solutions, talk versus action. Speeches don't put food on the table. Speeches don't fill up your tank, or fill your prescription, or do anything about that stack of bills that keeps you up at night.' He, on the other hand, had made capital from her decision to back the war in Iraq (a position she would later state she regretted) and in a televised debate he responded to a question about whether his opponent had sufficient likeability to become president with the double-edged compliment that she was 'likable enough'.

Once Obama had claimed the nomination, the process of rowing back from the animosity began. He did not want the fractious nomination battle to distract from his run for the presidency, and indeed his presidency itself, any longer than it needed to. Michelle, for instance, gave a speech at that year's Democratic Convention in which she praised 'people like Hillary Clinton, who put those 18 million cracks in the glass ceiling, so that our daughters – and sons – can dream a little bigger and aim a little higher'. Then Obama announced that she was his nominee for the prime position of Secretary of State – despite her initial reluctance to accept the position. She remained in the post for the duration of his first term and by the time she was contesting the 2016 presidential election, the Obama–Clinton relationship was on an apparently firm footing again. She would describe him as 'the man of hope' and said that 'America is stronger because of President Obama's leadership, and I'm better because of his friendship'. He, meanwhile, assured the electorate: 'I can say with confidence there has never been a man or a woman more qualified than Hillary Clinton to serve as president of the United States of America.' That Clinton became a great Obama ally, and not the thorn in his side that she might have had he opted to cut her out of his administration, is indicative of his alertness to seizing the initiative and taking control of a situation.

But to truly get inside the mind of Obama, it makes sense to look at specific policy areas over the next few sections to see what guiding principles underpinned them.

It's the Economy, Stupid

'We didn't become the most prosperous country in the world just by rewarding greed and recklessness. We didn't come this far by letting the special interests run wild. We didn't do it just by gambling and chasing paper profits on Wall Street. We built this country by making things, by producing goods we could sell.'

BARACK OBAMA, 2010

It was James Carville, Bill Clinton's campaign strategist during the 1992 presidential campaign, who popularized the phrase: 'The economy, stupid.' It was his contention that electoral success was dependent upon selling a message of credible economic hope. Persuade those in economic difficulties that you can make things better, and the world is your oyster.

It is a truism that for most governments in the developed world, the health of the economy is their primary aim, from which all else can follow. When Obama came to power, the political orthodoxy in the West for some thirty years had been that prosperity went hand in hand with a healthy financial sector largely left to its own devices. This was the model that Ronald Reagan and Margaret Thatcher had championed in the 1980s and which had largely persisted through much of the developed world.

But even as Obama made his run for the White House, the economic sands were fundamentally shifting. The Great Recession (see right) was just kicking in, dragging the USA and a host of other major nations into an economic downturn the like of which had not been seen since the Great Depression of the 1930s. Long-held assumptions about the resilience of financial institutions were suddenly thrown into doubt, and deep structural problems in our economic organization began to emerge. Obama was quick on to the case, laying out his plans even as he was becoming aware that the global economic crisis had the potential to blight his own tenure and suffocate his programme of change.

Underpinning his economic strategy was a fundamental belief that too many people were missing out on the rewards of an increasingly globalized economy because of rising rates of inequality. In a speech he gave at Osawatomie High School in Kansas in late 2011, he claimed America has the world's most productive workers and innovative companies. 'But for most Americans,' he warned, 'the basic bargain that made this country great has eroded. Long before the recession hit, hard work stopped paying off for too many people. Fewer and fewer of the folks who contributed to the success of our economy actually benefited from that success.' He pointed to some telling statistics in evidence – that in the previous few decades, the average income of the top 1 per cent has gone up by more than 250 per cent to US$1.2 million per year, while over the previous ten years the incomes of most Americans had fallen by 6 per cent; that the typical CEO who used to earn about thirty times more than their worker now earned 110 times more; and that some billionaires claimed a tax rate as low as 1 per cent.

THE GREAT RECESSION

The Great Recession was the global economic downturn that stemmed from the US subprime mortgage crisis of 2007. It was the culmination of years of lending by mortgage companies to individuals who couldn't afford their repayments, which left financial institutions dangerously exposed. In 2008 the investment bank, Lehman Brothers, went into liquidation, sparking fears of a meltdown in international markets. Banks considered 'too big to fail' without causing unacceptable levels of distress to the economy as a whole were expensively bailed out. Obama characterized it like this: 'We all know the story by now – mortgages sold to people who couldn't afford them … Banks and investors allowed to keep packaging the risk and selling it off. Huge bets – and huge bonuses – made with other people's money on the line. Regulators who … looked the other way or didn't have the authority to look at all.'

But while starting to address these problems, he knew that he first must act to ensure that the economy didn't go into immediate free fall. A month after taking office he signed off an economic stimulus package worth US$787 billion. Under its terms, money would go to healthcare, infrastructure development, education, tax breaks and incentives, and direct assistance to individuals – all in a bid to keep the economy bobbing along. Many interpreted it as a return to the economic doctrine of John Maynard Keynes, who argued that government spending was the most powerful response to economic crises and rising unemployment rates. Where Keynes's ideas had ruled during the Great Depression and after the Second World War (when numerous countries faced the task of economic rebuilding), his doctrine had been largely out of favour since the 1970s. But Obama seemed to be giving him a new seal of approval.

The fiscal stimulus ran alongside the Federal Reserve's programme of quantitative easing – whereby the Fed bought up financial assets so as to provide struggling financial institutions with the liquidity to keep the economy moving. Both tactics were highly controversial and measuring their results problematic. The level of investment demanded of the state was by any measure vast. But it is reasonable to suggest that the response of the Obama government fended off the very worst effects of the downturn that some commentators had feared unavoidable.

The situation also gave him some degree of licence to pursue reforms of the economic sector. While always keen to acknowledge the role of entrepreneurship and private business in achieving America's long-term economic pre-eminence, he could be scathing about under-regulated markets. Take, for example, these words from his 2009 inaugural address:

> Nor is the question before us whether the market is a force for good or ill. Its power to generate wealth and expand freedom is unmatched, but this crisis has reminded us that without a watchful eye, the market can spin out of control …

Or when he referenced one of his most esteemed forebears, Theodore Roosevelt:

> He was the Republican son of a wealthy family. He praised what the titans of industry had done to create jobs and grow the economy. He believed then what we know is true today, that the free market is the greatest force for economic progress in human history. It's led to a prosperity and a standard of living unmatched by the rest of the world. But Roosevelt also knew that the free market has never been a free license to take whatever you can from whomever you can.

He made the case for government intervention powerfully in a speech to Congress in 2009: '… the danger of too much government', he said, 'is matched by the perils of too little; that without the leavening hand of wise policy, markets can crash, monopolies can stifle competition, the vulnerable can be exploited …' A year later came the Dodd–Frank Wall

Street Reform and Consumer Protection Act that increased Wall Street regulation and, in Obama's words, would 'bring the shadowy deals that caused the crisis to the light of day' and 'put a stop to taxpayer bailouts once and for all'.

He advocated a fairer deal for ordinary workers, whom he extolled in his Labor Day speech of 2010:

> It was working men and women who made the twentieth century the American century. It was the labor movement that helped secure so much of what we take for granted today. The 40-hour work week, the minimum wage, family leave, health insurance, Social Security, Medicare, retirement plans. The cornerstones of middle-class security all bear the union label.

It was for them, he suggested, that financial sector regulatory reform was necessary. 'This isn't about class warfare,' he said in 2011. 'This is about the nation's welfare. It's about making choices that benefit not just the people who've done fantastically well over the last few decades, but that benefits the middle class, and those fighting to get into the middle class, and the economy as a whole.'

By the end of his presidency, the effects of the Great Recession were still being felt. However, the economy was back in growth mode and unemployment had not taken hold in the manner that it had done in the 1930s. There remained an underlying concern that the financial sector had not undergone the depth of reform necessary to avoid a repeat crisis but Obama was nonetheless able to finish his term on a note of cautious optimism, as when he said in his 2016 State of the Union address:

Let me start with the economy, and a basic fact: the United States of America, right now, has the strongest, most durable economy in the world. We're in the middle of the longest streak of private-sector job creation in history … For the past seven years, our goal has been a growing economy that works better for everybody. We've made progress. But we need to make more.

We are All Global Citizens

'The burdens of global citizenship continue
to bind us together… Partnership among nations is
not a choice; it is the one way, the only way,
to protect our common security and advance
our common humanity.'

BARACK OBAMA, 2008

Obama has made no secret of his patriotism and his belief that the United States represents values and offers opportunities that no other country can match. However, he has also made clear that he sees America within a global context – as a nation that must forge alliances, lead by example and, where necessary, intercede in the affairs of other countries. As the 'leader of the free world', he saw himself – and continues to do so – as part of the global community facing myriad problems that no nation alone can hope to solve. In the age of globalization, he advocated the need for international consensus not just in matters of foreign policy (which will be looked at in more detail later in this book) but – of perhaps more existential importance – in dealing with environmental challenges too.

Obama might rightly claim the title of America's first climate change president – the first to truly attempt to get to grips with the problem by substantially altering America's environmental practices.

His deep-felt concern for the future of the planet was evident in a talk he gave at Georgetown University in 2013:

That bright blue ball rising over the moon's surface, containing everything we hold dear – the laughter of children, a quiet sunset, all the hopes and dreams of posterity – that's what's at stake. That's what we're fighting for. And if we remember that, I'm absolutely sure we'll succeed.

As president, he was a champion of renewable energy, while simultaneously blocking a raft of drilling, mining and fracking projects that threatened an upsurge in the burning of fossil fuels and the degradation of valuable natural landscapes. His actions often met resistance from powerful financial interests but he nonetheless remained firm. He actively encouraged the development of renewable sources, as when in 2009 he signed off the American Recovery and Reinvestment Act that made available US$90 billion for renewable technology and clean transportation. Rob Sargent, senior director for the Campaign for 100% Renewable Energy, would say in 2016: 'President Obama and his Administration deserve tremendous kudos for jumpstarting America's clean energy revolution. Today we have twenty times more solar power and three times more wind energy compared to when he took office eight years ago … History will judge the Obama years as the turning point in America's shift to 100 per cent renewable energy.'

While the passage of domestic legislation has a positive impact on carbon emissions and sets a benchmark for other countries (and, to be clear, even under Obama's hand, America was a long way from the forefront of clean energy – a position generally considered to be held by Iceland, with 100 per cent renewable energy), Obama also recognized that the scale of the threat to the planet could only be addressed by international collaboration. He has expressed his frustration with those ideological and economic interests who dispute whether there really is an environmental threat on the scale suggested by the consensus of the international scientific community. In his speech at Georgetown, for example, he commented with exasperation: 'We don't have time for a meeting of the Flat Earth Society.' And at a speech in California a year later, he noted: 'It's pretty rare that you'll encounter somebody who says the problem you're trying to solve simply doesn't exist.'

Tackling environmental problems was front and centre of his agenda from the outset of his presidency. In his inauguration address, he acknowledged the particular duty of wealthy nations to set the pace. 'And to those nations like ours that enjoy relative plenty,' he said, 'we say we can no longer afford indifference to the suffering outside our borders; nor can we consume the world's resources without regard to effect. For the world has changed, and we must change with it.'

His single biggest contribution to the fight was the prominent role he played in securing the Paris Accord of 2015. After several years of negotiation, over 190 parties signed up to the climate change agreement that lays out several long-term goals, including restricting the increase in global average temperature to below 2°C compared to pre-industrial levels. Obama's impassioned but balanced address to the Paris Conference was regarded as a pivotal factor in swinging negotiations. He began by highlighting the cataclysmic threats of climate change: 'Submerged countries. Abandoned cities. Fields that no longer grow. Political disruptions that trigger new conflict, and even more floods of desperate peoples seeking the sanctuary of nations not their own.' But then he laid out his reasons for why there should be 'hope ... rooted in collective action ... united in common effort and by a common purpose'. He attacked the cynicism of opponents of the agreement, especially the attitude that there is nothing left to be done by humans to fight climate change. 'Last year, the global economy grew while global carbon emissions from burning fossil fuels stayed flat,' he explained. 'And what this means can't be overstated. We have broken the old arguments for inaction. We have proved that strong economic growth and a safer environment no longer have to conflict with one another; they can work in concert with one another.'

The final paragraph of his speech might also serve as a summary of his approach to the environment throughout his political career:

Our generation may not even live to see the full realization of what we do here. But the knowledge that the next generation will be better off for what we do here – can we imagine a more worthy reward than that? Passing that on to our children and our grandchildren, so that when they look back and they see what we did here in Paris, they can take pride in our achievement. Let that be the common purpose here in Paris. A world that is worthy of our children. A world that is marked not by conflict, but by cooperation; and not by human suffering, but by human progress. A world that's safer, and more prosperous, and more secure, and more free than the one that we inherited.

Expect the Unexpected

'Those of us who have had the singular privilege
to hold the office of the presidency know well that
progress in this country can be hard and it can be
slow, frustrating and sometimes you're stymied.'

BARACK OBAMA, 2014

Obama made the statement quoted on the previous page at the Lyndon B. Johnson Presidential Library Civil Rights Summit. It came in an address in which he was candid about the sense of vulnerability that attaches itself to the presidency. 'The office humbles you,' he said. 'You're reminded daily that in this great democracy, you are but a relay swimmer in the currents of history, bound by decisions made by those who came before, reliant on the efforts of those who will follow to fully vindicate your vision.'

Referring to the successes of the 1960s civil rights movement, and in particular the legislation passed by President Johnson, he warned against complacency. 'For history travels not only forwards,' he said, 'history can travel backwards, history can travel sideways. And securing the gains this country has made requires the vigilance of its citizens. Our rights, our freedoms – they are not given. They must be won. They must be nurtured through struggle and discipline, and persistence and faith.'

The sense of being subject to the currents of history was one that pervaded the Obama presidency. While very few leaders have the good fortune of a clear run in which they can see all that lies ahead of them, the Obama presidency was perhaps particularly prone to events beyond its control. Expecting the unexpected became an essential characteristic that he needed to develop to keep his tenure on track. At times he was forced down avenues that he would not have taken out of choice, his legislative programme was certainly knocked off-kilter on several occasions and he became a master of the compromise (see Don't be Afraid to Compromise on page 190). But while the 'unexpected' would stalk him, his preparedness to deal with it (to tackle what the former US Secretary of Defense, Donald Rumsfeld, might have referred to as the 'known unknowns', and the 'unknown unknowns') ensured his presidency was able to maintain its overall shape. His ability to deal with the shocks is a reflection of his innate pragmatism. As he told the Nobel Committee in 2009: 'We do not have to live in an idealized world to still reach for those ideals that will make it a better place.'

The 'unexpecteds' were already rearing up as Obama first campaigned for the White House. After a prolonged period of economic growth that survived even the effects of the 9/11 attacks of 2001, the economy had begun its tailspin. By the time he took office, he was confronted with a full-blown economic crisis that he could not have foreseen as he contemplated his run for the presidency. The task of averting financial Armageddon inevitably coloured his presidency – but that it did not knock it off its axis was an achievement of some magnitude. Throw in other largely unforeseeable crises – for instance, rising racial tensions amid a spate of filmed black deaths at the hands of police officers, or a threatened Ebola epidemic (which never actually materialized outside Africa) – and Obama's steadying hand becomes all the more evident.

In addition, there was an extensive list of unpredictable events on the international stage that required delicate handling. A non-exhaustive summary must include the fallout from the Arab Spring – including civil wars of varying magnitude in Egypt, Libya, Yemen and Syria – the Russian annexation of Crimea, and the rise of ISIS and its particularly brutal brand of terrorism. Obama turned to the wisdom of Martin Luther King under such circumstances, as when he referenced the following quotation:

> I refuse to accept despair as the final response to the ambiguities of history. I refuse to accept the idea that the 'isness' of man's present condition makes him morally incapable of reaching up for the eternal 'oughtness' that forever confronts him.

OBAMA'S NOBEL PRIZE

In 2009, less than a year into his presidency, Obama was awarded the Nobel Peace Prize for 'extraordinary efforts to strengthen international diplomacy and cooperation between peoples'. Many commentators were surprised by the award, not least Obama himself, who said that his own 'accomplishments are slight' and that he viewed it rather as 'an affirmation of American leadership on behalf of aspirations held by people in all nations' since. Nonetheless, it gave him the platform to outline his thoughts on the nature of war and peace, from his position – in his own words – as 'Commander-in-Chief of the military of a nation in the midst of two wars'. In his acceptance speech he talked of the need to 'think in new ways about the notions of just war and the imperatives of a just peace':

> For make no mistake: Evil does exist in the world. A nonviolent movement could not have halted Hitler's armies. Negotiations cannot convince al Qaeda's leaders to lay down their arms. To say that force may sometimes be necessary is not a call to cynicism – it is a recognition of history, the imperfections of man, and the limits of reason ... Only a just peace based on the inherent rights and dignity of every individual can truly be lasting ... But we must try as best we can to balance isolation and engagement, pressure and incentives, so that human rights and dignity are advanced over time.

Know When to Push Forward and When to Hold Back

'No system of government can or should be imposed by one nation on any other. That does not lessen my commitment, however, to governments that reflect the will of the people.'

BARACK OBAMA, 2009

Obama's foreign policy was one of the most divisive aspects of his time as president. He aimed to strike a delicate balance between, on the one hand, thrusting the US into other countries' affairs and, on the other, maintaining Washington's role as the international guardian of liberal democracy. Debate has raged as to what he managed to achieve, how it compared to what he promised, and what it was ever feasible for him to accomplish.

In terms of foreign policy positioning, Obama announced himself on the scene in 2002 with his speech in which he warned against the 'dumb war' in Iraq. He began by stating that he is not opposed to war in all circumstances, citing the American Civil War as one of the bloodiest in history yet necessary to 'drive the scourge of slavery from our soil'. Moreover, he said, in the aftermath of the 9/11 attacks he fully backed the Bush administration's pledge to 'hunt down and root out those who would slaughter innocents in the name of intolerance', adding that he 'would willingly take up arms myself to prevent such tragedy from happening again'. But he could not lend his backing to the Iraq invasion, which he prophetically predicted would end in a US occupation of undetermined length, at undetermined cost, with undetermined consequence. He critiqued the lack of a clear rationale and feared conflict would 'only fan the flames of the Middle East, and encourage the worst, rather than best, impulses of the Arab world'. He also pointedly suggested that it was time for the nation to wean itself off Middle Eastern oil 'through an energy policy that doesn't simply serve the interests of Exxon and Mobil'. In other words, he believed the war had an unacceptable economic element to its motivation. As a first major foray into foreign affairs, the speech pulled few punches.

By the time he was intent on running for the presidency, he was no less clear in setting out his goals. Take, for example, his address to the Jefferson–Jackson Day dinner in November 2007:

As President, I will end the war in Iraq. We will have our troops home in sixteen months. I will close Guantanamo. I will restore habeas corpus. I will finish the fight against Al Qaeda. And I will lead the world to combat the common threats of the 21st century – nuclear weapons and terrorism; climate change and poverty; genocide and disease. And I will send once more a message to those yearning faces beyond our shores that says, 'You matter to us. Your future is our future. And our moment is now.' America, our moment is now. Our moment is now.

Under his watch he pledged an end to the wars in Afghanistan and Iraq – which had, as he had predicted, taken on a life of their own – in favour of a more focused anti-terrorism policy. Addressing questions of nuclear proliferation, environmental threats and global poverty would constitute the other pillars of his foreign policy programme.

Against these standards, Obama enjoyed a number of successes. The US had withdrawn its forces from Iraq by the end of 2011, and although they returned in 2014 as that country descended into civil war, it was in a much reduced (aerial) role aimed at providing aid and countering the advance of Islamic State forces. Similarly, in Afghanistan combat operations drew to a close in 2014, although several thousand troops remain in the country to support Afghan forces and carry out counter-terrorism operations. As for leading the fight against international terrorism, Obama's single greatest triumph was to okay the missions that located and killed off Osama bin Laden, the mastermind behind the 9/11 attacks.

As we have already seen, Obama's central role in the adoption of the Paris Accord marked a major success in the international fight against climate change. Furthermore, the Joint Comprehensive Plan of Action agreed between Iran on one side and the EU, China, France, Russia, the UK and the US on the other, represented his standout achievement in dealing with the global nuclear threat. The culmination of some two years of negotiations, the deal saw Iran pledge to reduce its uranium stockpiles

---

THE DEATH OF OSAMA BIN LADEN

Obama was determined to pursue those who posed terrorist threats to the US. In his 2009 inauguration address, he said: 'We will not apologize for our way of life, nor will we waver in its defense, and for those who seek to advance their aims by inducing terror and slaughtering innocents, we say to you now that our spirit is stronger and cannot be broken; you cannot outlast us, and we will defeat you.' He was particularly eager for the capture of Osama bin Laden, and the opportunity came when bin Laden was tracked down to the Pakistani city of Abbottabad. Apparently without the foreknowledge of Pakistan's government, Obama authorized a Special Operations Unit to launch a raid under cover of darkness on 2 May 2011. Bin Laden was killed and Obama soberly addressed the nation: 'Justice has been done.'

---

and restrict its nuclear research programme for fifteen years in return for the lifting of sanctions. Imperfect as the deal was – principally for its non-permanence – it was widely celebrated as a triumph of diplomacy by the international community. There was also good progress towards the normalizing of relations with Cuba in what became known as 'the Cuban Thaw', following decades of bad blood between the two countries.

But for the successes and steps forwards, there were plenty of knock-backs too. Most notably, perhaps, it quickly became apparent that the Arab Spring that began in 2011 in a blaze of hope was merely the first act in a prolonged phase of regional upheaval that involved a complex and disparate set of interests. The initial sense that the protests had advanced the cause of liberal democracy soon faded. US military support for rebels intent on the overthrow of Colonel Gaddafi in Libya originally seemed to have met its goal when he was ousted but civil discord quickly overcame the nation. Then, in 2012, militants from the Ansar al-Sharia group launched attacks on US government facilities in Benghazi, killing several people including the US ambassador, J. Christopher Stevens. It was another devastating blow to the US psyche and may be regarded as a spur to those who have subsequently pushed a far more isolationist agenda. For Obama, it was an incident that came to haunt his presidency as his opponents alleged improper conduct by the Washington administration, including refusing to grant extra security to American facilities prior to the attack.

America's diplomatic interventions in Yemen also failed to deliver the desired results as that country too spiralled into chaos. But most devastating of all was Syria (see box on page 155). Unable to martial an international response to the excesses of Assad, Obama soon found himself being drawn into the quagmire of a battlefield in which atrocities became the stock-in-trade of all sides fighting on the ground. Moreover, his inability to bring Assad to task over his use of chemical weapons (see You Can't Always Get What You Want on page 184) seriously called into question his ability to follow through on his promises at the international level. The Syrian collapse left Obama a diminished figure in the eyes of many foreign affairs commentators.

Furthermore, the regional disruption that proceeded from the Arab Spring proved a fertile breeding ground for emerging militant groups – Islamic State being the most notorious. Obama's use of tactics including Special Operations Units and drone strikes perhaps represented the 'cleanest' methods of flushing out terrorist threats but nonetheless provided the very groups it was targeting with powerful propaganda material. While Obama was undoubtedly correct not to go full throttle into a series of 'dumb wars' that he couldn't hope to win, the at-a-distance interventions of the US did little to bring the Western and Arab spheres closer together. Nor did his tenure see any significant progress towards solving the Israeli–Palestinian question. Throw in the relative powerlessness of the West in general, and the USA in particular, to do anything substantive in the face of Russia's 2014 annexation of Crimea (previously a sovereign region of Ukraine), and the sense grows that Obama never quite mastered steering the US's role as the world's policeman.

Yet to the end, Obama remained true to his original ideals: to strike back against active enemies, to seek

THE SYRIA CONUNDRUM

By 2017 the Syrian Civil War had killed an estimated 400,000 people, forced over 5 million into exile and rendered millions more internally displaced. The conflict emerged from the Arab Spring, which in Syria manifested as large-scale protests against the rule of President Bashar al-Assad. After Assad resisted early pressure from the international community to stand down, fighting became entrenched as disparate interests were embroiled in the conflict. Among them were the forces of Assad and his international allies, Kurdish, Sunni and Salafi militants, the Islamic State group, Turkish fighters supporting various opposition groups, and a US-led coalition moving against targets on both the government and Islamic State sides. It has the hallmarks of being the most devastating and intractable conflict of the age – a tragic legacy given that when Assad took power in 2000 there were high hopes that the Western-educated leader might initiate democratic reforms.

peaceable routes to ending conflicts, and to support free and fair governments. Addressing the UN General Assembly in New York in 2016, he spoke of maintaining the 'commitment to international cooperation rooted in the rights and responsibilities of nations'. He continued:

> Our international community must continue to work with those who seek to build rather than to destroy … Sometimes I'm criticized in my own country for professing a belief in international norms and multilateral institutions. But I am convinced that in the long run, giving up some freedom of action – not giving up our ability to protect ourselves or pursue our core interests, but binding ourselves to international rules over the long term – enhances our security. And I think that's not just true for us.

Yet for all the good intentions, Stephen M. Walt, writing on ForeignPolicy.com in early 2017, could provide only this scathing summary of Obama's foreign doctrine: 'But in foreign policy Obama's record was mostly one of failure. Neither the state of the world nor America's position in it is stronger today than they were when he took office.'

Obama and God

'… without a vessel for my beliefs, without a commitment to a particular community of faith, at some level I would always remain apart, and alone.'

BARACK OBAMA, 2006

For a country built upon the principle that Church and State ought to be separate, religion continues to play a vital role in American life – both in the public and private spheres. According to the Pew Research Centre, almost 60 per cent of Americans say religion plays a very important role in their lives – by some distance the highest rate among major developed nations. So the question of Obama's own religious convictions as he first sought and then executed high office was of major significance, even more so in an era when the rise of Islamist extremism has exacerbated religious tensions. Throughout his time in the public eye, he has professed his profound Christian beliefs while also espousing a liberal social agenda that has not always sat well with the nation's large pool of Christian conservatives.

Crucially, he has repeatedly emphasized his support for the principle of freedom of religion – the right to freely and peaceably practise one's religious beliefs without fear of prejudice or government intervention. In an age of acute religious disharmony – most notably, in the West, a pronounced increase in Islamophobia – he worked hard to foster interreligious harmony. Consider, for instance, his commencement address at Indiana's Catholic University of Notre Dame in 2009:

> For if there is one law that we can be most certain of, it is the law that binds people of all faiths and no faith together. It's no coincidence that it exists in Christianity and Judaism; in Islam and Hinduism; in Buddhism and humanism. It is, of course, the Golden Rule – the call to treat one another as we wish to be treated. The call to love. The call to serve. To do what we can to make a difference in the lives of those with whom we share the same brief moment on this Earth.

Obama was not brought up in a religious household. His mother was sceptical of organized religion, while his maternal grandparents were non-practising Baptists and Methodists. His father, on the other hand, was born Muslim but became an atheist. Obama's religious life thus only started in earnest after he moved to Chicago and began working for a community organization affiliated to a Christian church. It was in this period that he developed a sense that there was something missing in his life. In 2006 he told an audience at a Christian conference in Washington DC:

> It was because of these newfound understandings that I was finally able to walk down the aisle of Trinity United Church of Christ on 95th Street in the Southside of Chicago one day and affirm my

Christian faith. It came about as a choice, and not an epiphany. I didn't fall out in church. The questions I had didn't magically disappear. But kneeling beneath that cross on the South Side, I felt that I heard God's spirit beckoning me.

He went on to speak of how he believed religion gave those who, like him, felt they had lost a 'sense of purpose, a narrative arc to their lives'. He also emphasized that professing religious conviction does not imply that you 'don't have doubts'. Doubt, he argued, is actually a crucial aspect of the religious experience. 'You need to come to church in the first place,' he said, 'precisely because you are first of this world, not apart from it.' This idea that religious belief is a process rather than a fixed position would inform his outlook as president at a time when unbending religious fanaticism was finding expression in a wave of militancy that has claimed hundreds of thousands of lives throughout the world.

It is Obama's contention that religious discourse in the public sphere is vital to countering the rise of religious extremism. This was a particularly striking position for a president from the Democratic Party, many of whose socially liberal supporters have long regarded religion as a subject best left out of political debate. Obama said of their stance on religion in 2006:

At best, we may try to avoid the conversation about religious values altogether, fearful of offending anyone and claiming that – regardless of our personal beliefs – constitutional principles tie our hands. At worst, there are some liberals who dismiss religion in the public square as inherently irrational or intolerant, insisting on a caricature of religious Americans that paints them as fanatical, or thinking that the very word 'Christian' describes one's political opponents, not people of faith.

He explained that he considered it a mistake to fail to acknowledge the power of faith in people's lives, or to ignore questions of how to reconcile faith with a modern, pluralistic democracy.

In *The Audacity of Hope*, he warned against political actors abandoning the field of religious discourse, or discussing religion solely in negative terms of 'where or how it should not be practiced, rather than in the positive sense of what it tells us about our obligations toward one another'. To do so, he said, is to create a vacuum that will be filled by 'those with the most insular views of faith, or who cynically use religion to justify partisan ends'. His hope, as he told that Washington conference in 2006, is instead that 'we can live with one another in a way that reconciles the beliefs of each with the good of all'.

THE JEREMIAH WRIGHT AFFAIR

Briefly, the issue of religion threatened to derail Obama's first run for the presidency. Jeremiah Wright was a pastor in Chicago and a mentor to Obama from the 1980s (providing him with the famous phrase, 'the audacity of hope'). But in March 2008 a number of controversial sermons came to light. Wright had suggested that the 9/11 attacks represented 'America's chickens … coming home to roost' and he accused the government of a history of lying in relation to the mistreatment of non-whites. Obama sought to distance himself from the scandal – stating that 'words that degrade individuals have no place in our public dialogue' – but his critics were not satisfied. Obama fought back with what became known as the 'A More Perfect Union' address. Condemning Wright's words but putting them in the context of America's history of race relations, and while not satisfying everyone, it bought him the goodwill to move on from this most divisive of episodes.

Religion Can be a Driver of Social Cohesion

'We can discuss the religious call to address poverty and environmental stewardship all we want, but it won't have an impact unless we tackle head-on the mutual suspicion that sometimes exists between religious America and secular America.'

BARACK OBAMA, 2006

Part of Obama's affinity with the Christian Church rests in his belief that the Church itself can be a powerful vehicle for delivering social good. After all, social work in Chicago was a vital aspect of his own coming into the Church. He has also cited the role of the Church in the fight for black civil rights – something he has referred to as 'the power of the African-American religious tradition to spur social change'. Because of its history, he argued, 'the black church understands in an intimate way the biblical call to feed the hungry and clothe the naked and challenge powers and principalities'. By playing such a prominent role in historical struggles for freedom and the rights of man, he said in 2006, faith serves as more than merely 'a comfort to the weary or a hedge against death, but rather as an active, palpable agent in the world. As a source of hope.'

Rather than sidelining religious debate for fear of 'getting "preachy"', he believes that there should be greater public exploration of how religious values and culture can be harnessed to address society's most urgent social problems. He had thus accused secularists of being wrong in asking believers to 'leave their religion at the door before entering into the public square'. Citing such notable figures as Abraham Lincoln, Dorothy Day (a radical Catholic social activist) and Martin Luther King, he contends that 'to say that men and women should not inject their "personal morality" into public policy debates is a practical absurdity'.

That is not to say, however, that he believes people of religious conviction necessarily have a greater claim to moral rectitude. Speaking in 2006, he said: 'I would rather have someone who is grounded in morality and ethics, and who is also secular, affirm their morality and ethics and values without pretending that they're something they're not.' He also made it clear that he believes that while some aspects of Christian faith are unchanging – for instance, belief in the Ten Commandments and Christ's divinity – others are rooted in a specific cultural milieu and can be modified in accordance with prevailing currents of opinion.

He illustrated the point with reference to the vexed issue of abortion. In the 2004 race for the Illinois Senate, his opponent, Alan Keyes, claimed that 'Jesus Christ would not vote for Barack Obama' because he had refused to back a package of anti-abortion laws. Obama responded by arguing that while an individual might be opposed to abortion for religious reasons, a change in the law could not be leveraged simply by pointing to the teaching of a given church or by evoking 'God's will'. Instead, it must be shown that abortion violates some principle accessible to people of all faiths and no faith at all. Within a diverse society such as America's, he said, 'Politics depends on our ability to persuade each other of common aims based on a common reality.'

BRIDGING THE RELIGIOUS DIVIDE

In June 2009 Obama gave one of the most notable speeches of his presidency to an audience at Egypt's Cairo University. It was an appeal for America and the Muslim world to start healing the wounds that had been festering for several years. 'I've come here to Cairo to seek a new beginning between the United States and Muslims around the world,' he said, '… one based upon the truth that America and Islam are not exclusive and need not be in competition … There must be a sustained effort to listen to each other; to learn from each other; to respect one another; and to seek common ground.' In 2015, Obama again addressed the question of interfaith harmony, controversially warning Christians not to 'get on our high horse' given a record that includes the Crusades, the Inquisition and slavery. A committed Christian personally, his desire to reach out to other faiths has been striking.

Religion Can be a Driver of Social Cohesion

Obama cherishes the sanctity of the USA's pluralistic status and the separation of Church and State, which he says has been crucial not only to preserving democracy, but also to protecting the robustness of religious practice. It is a country, after all, that was founded by those escaping religious persecution in Europe. Thus while acknowledging 'the role my faith has in guiding my own values and my own beliefs', he fiercely defends the rights of others to follow any (or no) faith of their choosing. As he told the Islamic Society of Baltimore in January 2016: '… if we're serious about freedom of religion … we have to understand an attack on one faith is an attack on all our faiths'.

All Work and
No Play …

'There was a game where I scored twenty-seven
points. That was a pretty good week.'

BARACK OBAMA, 2015

Obama made the statement on the previous page when listing 'the best weeks of his life' in response to a journalist's question. The sport to which he referred was basketball – a game he has enjoyed since his youth and one for which his rangy, lithe form is ideal. It is a pastime that he continued to indulge in throughout his time as president. In a podcast with Marc Maron in 2015, he said:

> I was never great, but I was a good player and I could play seriously. Now I'm one of these old guys who's running around. The guys I play with – who are all a lot younger – they sorta pity me and sympathize with me. They tolerate me, but we all know I'm the weak link on the court and I don't like being the weak link.

Making time for some relaxation was a notable feature of his presidency and served several purposes. Firstly, it allowed for at least some downtime and normality, for him and for the family as a whole – an opportunity for leisure and recreation in the interests of mental well-being. One of his first presidential orders was to have the White House tennis court converted for use as a basketball court too. Moreover, it helped cement Obama's image as essentially a regular guy – one of us.

Although basketball is his great sporting love (and the Chicago Bulls his favoured team), he enjoys other sports, too. He is a runner, and in his younger years at Columbia he would regularly run three miles a day. He is also a keen golfer and is reputed to have played more while in office than any other president since Dwight Eisenhower. Sometimes his devotion to the game brought criticism from those who felt he should be spending his time on more pressing issues. But in an address to journalists at a Gridiron Club dinner in 2011, Obama pithily dismissed the idea that golf represented time wasted. 'And for all those who think I golf too much,' he said, 'let me be clear. I'm not spending time on the golf course – I'm investing time on the golf course.' Rather more sedately, he is also known to be keen on the occasional game of pool.

While some may regard such hobbies as frivolous, Obama nonetheless sees real value in sports. There are the obvious health benefits, which fed into his wife's 'Let's Move' campaign. But he also recognizes their role in breaking down barriers. In a speech at the White House in his last week in office, he said:

> It is worth remembering – because sometimes people wonder, 'Well, why are you spending time on sports? There's other stuff going on' – throughout our history, sports have had this power to bring us together, even

when the country is divided. Sports have changed attitudes and culture in ways that seem subtle but that ultimately made us think differently about ourselves and who we were. It is a game, and it is a celebration, but there's a direct line between Jackie Robinson and me standing here ... And sports have a way, sometimes, of changing hearts in a way that politics or business doesn't. And sometimes it's just a matter of us being able to escape and relax from the difficulties of our days, but sometimes it also speaks to something better.

Having burned off the calories in sporting endeavour, Obama was also able to indulge his love of food. His culinary passions held an enduring fascination for political commentators. He is known as a passionate devourer of junk food, delighting in good-quality burgers, pizzas and hot dogs (although he has expressly stated that the last should not be served with tomato ketchup to anyone over the age of eight), with ice cream his pudding of choice. For snacking, he has a predilection for chips and guacamole as well as chocolate-covered macadamias and peanuts. He even had the White House brew its own beer – although he consumes little alcohol himself and has listed Black Forest Berry iced tea as his preferred drink.

But, fittingly for a president who urged the nation to eat more healthily, he also embraces food with higher nutritional value. Michelle's shrimp linguini is a known favourite while his own speciality is chilli. He also enjoys salmon and broccoli (which he has claimed is his favourite vegetable and which presumably was harvested during the presidency from his wife's fabled vegetable patch). There was always a bowl of apples to hand in the Oval Office, too. On the downside, he was a prodigious smoker – a favoured method of relaxing that went down less well with his wife. It is said he promised to quit in return for her support of his 2008 run for the White House, but fell off the wagon until giving up for good in 2010 'because I'm scared of my wife'.

Obama also likes to give his brain a workout by playing word puzzles, as well as Scrabble and poker. He is a fan of the arts in their many forms too, recognizing their power for both the individual and society in general. His love of music is explored in the next section, but in addition he enjoys drawing (he refers to himself as a 'doodler' and nominates Picasso as his favourite artist) and cinema (with *Casablanca* and *One Flew Over the Cuckoo's Nest* his go-to movies). He is also a keen fan of comics, having collected editions of *Spider-Man* and *Conan the Barbarian* over the years. In a speech in Vietnam in 2016, he gave an impassioned defence of the right of everyone to freely explore the arts. 'Look, let's be honest,' he said, 'sometimes art is dangerous though, and that's why governments sometimes get nervous about art. But one of the things that I truly believe is that if you try to suppress the arts then I think you're suppressing the deepest dreams and aspirations of a people.'

Obama's Taste
in Music

'If you swiped through my music collection, you'd
find some Bruce, some Stevie, some Al Green.'

BARACK OBAMA, 2016

Although not a musician in the mould of such White House predecessors as Richard Nixon (pianist) or Bill Clinton (saxophonist), music provided a thread that ran throughout the Obama presidency. Not only was he ready to share his personal music tastes with the world (including, in the later years of his presidency, an annual update on the new music he had been listening to), but he also provided some memorable musical interludes of his own.

Two instances stand out. The first came in 2012 when Obama serenaded soul legend Al Green, who was in attendance at a presidential event, with an impromptu rendition of Green's own 'Let's Stay Together'. Then, in 2015 at the memorial service for Clementa C. Pinckney, one of the victims of a shooting in Charleston in 2015, he sang an a cappella version of 'Amazing Grace' in a performance of both panache and poignancy. The British classical music radio station Classic FM would subsequently praise his performances, noting that 'there might be something resembling perfect pitch (or at least great intuition) in Obama's musical arsenal' and describing the intensity and confidence of his 'Amazing Grace' as 'absolutely bang-on'. As well as his vocal abilities, Obama has also garnered a reputation as a dancer, from tango and salsa to dancing the lipala in Kenya and partaking in what he refers to as 'dad moves'.

That performance at the Pinckney memorial service illustrated his understanding of just how powerful music can be. At a time of heightened racial tensions, his singing undercut those strains as effectively as the address that accompanied it. In part, this is because music transcends racial boundaries – nowhere more so than in America, where traditionally 'black' musical forms including jazz, gospel and spirituals have paved the way for the modern mainstream genres of soul, pop, rap and R&B. At a gospel concert held at the White House in 2015, he gave a nod to the links between the nation's music and its history when he traced the roots of gospel to the spirituals sung by slaves. 'Songs were where their dreams took flight,' he said, 'where they expressed faith and love, as well as pain and fear and unimaginable loss. They sang songs of liberation, if not for their bodies in this world, then for their souls in the next.' In another speech, he spoke of the role of music in forming the US identity. 'We're the inventors of gospel and jazz and blues,' he said, 'bluegrass and country, and hip-hop and rock and roll, and our very own sound with all the sweet sorrow and reckless joy of freedom.'

As for his own tastes, eclectic is the word. 'If I had one musical hero, it would have to be Stevie Wonder,' he once told *Rolling Stone* magazine. 'When I was at that point where you start getting involved in music, Stevie had that run with *Music of My Mind, Talking Book, Fulfillingness' First Finale* and *Innervisions*, and then *Songs in the Key of Life*. Those are as brilliant a set of five albums as we've ever seen.' Being a teenager in the seventies, he was listening to heavyweights including Elton John, Earth, Wind & Fire, and the Rolling Stones ('Gimme Shelter' being his favourite of their tracks). Dylan is another favourite, with 1975's *Blood on the Tracks* especially popular with Obama. However, when he is in the midst of the political season he particularly enjoys Dylan's 1965 song, 'Maggie's Farm'. 'It speaks to me as I listen to some of the political rhetoric,' he has said.

Dylan accounts for around thirty tracks on Obama's musical playlist but there is much else besides. In his own words, he listens to 'everything from Howlin' Wolf to Yo-Yo Ma to Sheryl Crow'. Indubitably, much of his preferred listening reveals he is a man of a certain age. His favourites include Miles Davis, Aretha Franklin, John Coltrane, Van Morrison, Ray Charles, Frank Sinatra, Count Basie, Leonard Cohen, Joni Mitchell, Nina Simone, Otis Redding, the Temptations, the Isley Brothers, Bob Marley and the Wailers, and Sly and the Family Stone. But there are also artists of more recent vintage, from Coldplay and the Fugees to John Legend, Justin Timberlake, and Florence and the Machine.

He has proved skilled at tapping into the current of contemporary music to spread his political message. He has socialized with the likes of Ludacris and Usher, while will.i.am's 'Yes We Can' (based on Obama's electoral slogan) was a massive internet sensation on its release in 2008. But it is perhaps Jay-Z whose musical career most reflects Obama's political ascent. To millions, Jay-Z has built an artistic and commercial empire that proves the American dream is still achievable. Obama has even referenced the rapper in campaign speeches ('Dirt Off Your Shoulder' serving as a metaphor for his attitude to criticisms thrown at him by opponents) and has said of him: 'Every time I talk to Jay-Z, who is a brilliant talent and a good guy, I enjoy how he thinks. He's serious and he cares about his art. That's somebody who is going to start branching out and can help shape attitudes in a real, positive way.' Obama thus sees music not only in terms of pleasure and a release but as a potent agent of change, too.

Healthcare for All

'I want to stop talking about the outrage of 47
million Americans without health care and start
actually doing something about it.'

BARACK OBAMA, 2007

Reforming the American healthcare system was always a key priority for Obama. As president, it would become his primary focus once he had pushed through the economic stimulus package that he deemed essential to deal with the financial crisis. It was a brave move on Obama's part because he knew that he would have a battle on his hands to convince not only his political opponents that reform was needed but large contingents of the public too.

To Obama and many of his supporters, the case for expanding medical insurance was straightforward. Before he introduced his reforms, planning for healthcare was an ordeal for many. If you were lucky, your employer provided your coverage but that left many corporate workers feeling tied into their jobs and unable to branch out alone for fear of not being able to afford their own health cover. The less fortunate faced the unenviable task of financing insurance themselves, unless they were covered by the government Medicaid programme (offering limited assistance to those on low incomes) or else Medicare (a national health insurance programme for qualifying over-sixty-fives and those fulfilling a narrow band of other qualifying conditions).

Moreover, many of those with pre-existing conditions – those, it might be said, most in need – were routinely denied coverage or else quoted prohibitive premiums. Others did not take recommended screenings – for instance, for breast cancer – for fear of causing their premiums to rocket. The stark situation in 2010 was that some 48 million Americans lacked health insurance. The Democratic Party had been attempting to introduce changes to the system for decades, though largely ineffectually. Serious illness or injury represented one of two things to many of the uninsured – either serious financial impoverishment as they attempted to pay large medical bills from their own resources, or else a future coping (or not addressing) pressing medical concerns.

For Obama, such a situation was simply unacceptable in a country as wealthy and socially developed as the USA. As he reflected in 2016 in a speech at Miami Dade College:

> One thing I want to start with is just reminding people why it is that we fought for health reform in the first place. Because it was one of the key motivators in my campaign. And it wasn't just because rising health costs were eating into workers' pay checks and straining budgets for businesses and for governments. It wasn't just because, before the law was passed, insurance companies could just drop your coverage because you got sick, right at the time you needed insurance most. It was because of you. It was because of the stories that I was hearing all around the country, and right here in

Florida — hearing from people who had been forced to fight a broken healthcare system at the same time as they were fighting to get well. It was about children like Zoe Lihn, who needed heart surgery when she was just 15 hours old — just a baby, just an infant. And she was halfway to hitting her lifetime insurance cap before she was old enough to walk.

Obama's plan was to drive through an Affordable Care Act (popularly known as Obamacare) to guarantee affordable health insurance for all. This was to be done principally through a combination of tax credits for those taking up government-sponsored health insurance plans, and by expanding Medicaid. There were new regulations for insurance companies too, notably a ban on punitive measures against sufferers of pre-existing conditions and a prohibition on higher premiums, as had often been the case, for women.

Yet there was a significant body of opposition highly sceptical that the government should increase its role in healthcare provision. This was, critics suggested, an overstretch by Big Government, or even the first step down a path to socialism. The tax increases for businesses needed to subsidize the plans would result in job losses, they said, or else everyone would be forced to take up Obamacare, regardless of personal preferences. There would be rationing, doctors forced to decide who they could afford to let live and die, federal bankruptcy … there was no shortage of apocalyptic scenarios offered up.

It was initially Obama's intention to let each house of Congress draft its own legislation with cross-party cooperation. It would be a way, he hoped, to ensure reform by consensus. In practice, he encountered massive pushback from Republicans who wouldn't countenance getting on board with Obama's vision. Obamacare was passed by the Senate in December 2009 and by the House of Representatives in March 2010 without the support of a single Republican. It was a bruising experience for the still relatively new president but he was determined to get his reforms through. Still they would face legal challenges, not to mention the constant threat that a future Republican administration might roll them back.

Of the 80 per cent or so of people who had previously had workplace insurance, the impact of Obamacare was limited, save that premiums grew more slowly under the new system. There were hiccups too, most notably technical problems with the introduction of an online government portal in 2013 – a mishap opponents gleefully seized upon. But for those who had previously been uninsured, its effects were clearer. In the six years to 2016, the number of uninsured fell from 48 million to 28.5 million. Obama noted: 'The Affordable Care Act has done what it was designed to do: It gave us affordable healthcare.'

Obamacare qualifies as one of the outstanding successes of his domestic legislative programme. It is, of course, by no means perfect. Aside from administrative and technological problems, and the direct cost to government, a small proportion of people (estimated at around 3 per cent) – mostly those privately buying cover directly from insurance companies – found their premiums rose. But for most, costs stayed constant or fell. More pertinently, by 2016 only around 10 per cent of the population was uninsured, compare to around 20 per cent in 2010. As for Obama, he was perhaps never more dogged than in pursuit of these reforms, nor more ready to show his teeth. The passage of Obamacare marked him out as a president who would take on even the most ferocious of opposition for what he truly believes in.

In his own words from 2016:

> This is more than just about healthcare. It's about the character of our country. It's about whether we look out for one another. It's about whether the wealthiest nation on earth is going to make sure that nobody suffers. Nobody loses everything they have saved, everything they have worked for because they're sick. You stood up for the idea that no American should have to go without the healthcare they need.

You Can't Always Get What You Want

'Democracy in a nation of more than 300 million people is inherently difficult. It's always been noisy and messy, contentious, complicated.'

BARACK OBAMA, 2010

Obamacare was perhaps the prime example of Obama's ability to drive through policy in which he truly believes, by a mixture of force of will and wily political operation. Yet at other times, he was forced to accept defeat. His tenure was pockmarked by occasions when he was compelled to row back from his desired course of action because of lack of support, either from Congress or the public at large.

One such episode occurred in 2012 in relation to Obama's so-called Syrian 'red line'. With Syria by then descending into civil war after President Assad launched a crackdown on his opponents in light of the previous year's popular protests, it was widely accepted that the Syrian government possessed a stockpile of chemical weapons. Obama responded by saying that the deployment of chemical weapons would be to cross a 'red line' prompting 'enormous consequences'.

In 2013, it was reliably alleged that Assad had authorized toxic gas attacks on locations close to Damascus, killing some 1,400 people including over 400 children. The red line had been definitively crossed and Obama was under pressure to act. If he did not, his utterances from the previous year would count as nothing but empty promises. Those on the international stage who relied on US protection would feel more vulnerable, while America's enemies would surely be fortified.

Plans were put in place for a joint US–UK–French response in the form of air strikes on strategic Syrian targets. But the putative operation soon unravelled. The British parliament voted against such action and Obama, realizing that he could not rely on the support of Congress or a public still reeling from the country's prolonged involvement in Afghanistan and Iraq, also backed down. France had little choice but to follow suit, with President François Hollande bemoaning 'a missed opportunity that could have changed the course of the war'. It was certainly a humiliation for Obama, with some commentators suggesting that the US's international reputation had been seriously dented.

Diplomatic efforts, in combination with Russia, did see Syria sign up to the Organization for the Prohibition of Chemical Weapons and agree to the removal of a large part of its chemical arsenal. Nonetheless, further suspected gas attacks cemented the idea that this had been a bad defeat for the Obama presidency. More recently, it has been posited that Obama held off a more aggressive response in order to keep Syria's ally, Iran, onside at a critical moment in the negotiations towards the 2015 agreement on ending its nuclear activities. Even if that were true – and its veracity is disputed – the affair left Obama battered. Where he had been prepared to put his neck on the line for a cause like Obamacare (a project which, in his view, would save lives), he did not feel able to do the same when at stake was a policy that would likely result in deaths. For that, he demanded backing which was not sufficiently there.

A knock-back on a par with the Syrian 'red line' was the failure to close Guantanamo Bay, the controversial detention centre located off the coast of Cuba. It had been established in 2002 by the Bush administration in the early days of the so-called War on Terror to hold those identified as combatants against the US. The prison gained a reputation for detaining some prisoners for years without recourse to a trial, and there were also allegations of torture. During his first campaign for the presidency and throughout the early days of his tenure, Obama made clear his intention to close the facility. As he told an audience at Cairo University in 2009:

Nine-eleven was an enormous trauma to our country. The fear and anger that it provoked was understandable. But in some cases, it led us to act contrary to our traditions and our ideals. We are taking concrete actions to change course. I have unequivocally prohibited the use of torture by the United States. And I have ordered the prison at Guantanamo Bay closed by early next year.

Yet as he handed over office to Donald Trump in 2017, Guantanamo Bay remained stubbornly open, even if the number of prisoners had decreased from 245 when Obama came to office to forty-one. Where he had once assumed he would be able to garner sufficient cross-party support for the closure, it never proved to be the case. There was neither the appetite to hold suspected terrorists and other enemies of the state on US soil, nor a willingness to pay for the high-security facilities needed to house them. Moreover, the Pentagon never wholeheartedly backed the plan and the energies of Obama's staff were also absorbed in pursuit of other key policy objectives such as Obamacare. As the end of his presidency lurched into view, Obama was still making the case for closure. In 2016 he described the camp as 'contrary to our values. It undermines our standing in the world. It is viewed as a stain on our broader record of upholding the highest standards of rule of law.' Certainly he left it a much smaller concern than at its peak when it held hundreds of prisoners, but he would have wished it was not there at all when Trump came to power – Trump quickly announced his intention to keep the camp open indefinitely. Once again, on an issue related to national defence, Obama was unable to carry the day.

BYPASSING CONGRESS

US presidents have several weapons in their arsenal when unable to carry Congress with them. The president, for instance, has the right to issue executive orders – which effectively carry the weight of a law although may not be used to bypass Congress on major policy areas – as well as presidential proclamations, national security directives and memoranda. These allow the president to affect matters of internal government, mould the roll-out of certain legislation and ensure steady government in times of crisis and war. Back in 2008 Obama had spoken out against White House incumbent George W. Bush's use of such instruments, commenting: 'The biggest problems that we're facing right now have to do with George Bush trying to bring more and more power into the executive branch and not go through Congress at all.' But once in power, and faced with a regularly hostile Republican Party in Congress, Obama employed them too – in fact, he implemented some 50 per cent more administrative regulations than Bush. 'Now, I am going to be working with Congress where I can,' he said in 2014, '… but I'm going to act on my own if Congress is deadlocked. I've got a pen to take executive actions where Congress won't…' He issued, for example, directives on the use of torture, the minimum wage for federal employees and rights for LGBT workers. As John F. Kennedy once observed: 'Many things can be done by a stroke of the presidential pen.'

Don't be Afraid to Compromise

'And what the American people hope – what
they deserve – is for all of us, Democrats and
Republicans, to work through our differences; to
overcome the numbing weight of our politics.'

BARACK OBAMA, STATE OF THE
UNION ADDRESS, 2010

As already seen, Obama fundamentally believed in Congress-led government and could only do so much unilaterally. But, of course, he faced an often highly resistant Republican opposition that, after the 2014 midterms, controlled both houses. Yet still he strived to win the big arguments. In 2006 he had said: 'Politics depends on our ability to persuade each other of common aims based on a common reality. It involves the compromise, the art of what's possible.' It was a sentiment he never gave up on.

At times, it proved a hugely frustrating edict to follow. At Ted Kennedy's memorial service in 2009, he harked back to an earlier age 'when the joy and nobility of politics prevented differences of party and philosophy from becoming barriers to cooperation and mutual respect – a time when adversaries still saw each other as patriots'.

His sense that modern Washington had lost that ethos of mutual respect was palpable. As early as 2006 he had written in a fundraising letter that 'what Washington needs is adult supervision' and five years later he confided to the press: 'You want everybody to act like adults, quit playing games, realize it's not just "my way or the highway".' By 2013, at the culmination of a government shutdown (see page 194), his tone was even more strained:

> Those of us who have the privilege to serve this country have an obligation to do our job as best we can. We come from different parties, but we are Americans first. And that's why disagreement cannot mean dysfunction. It can't degenerate into hatred. The American people's hopes and dreams are what matter, not ours. Our obligations are to them.

His commitment to engaging his opponents in debate never wavered, though, nor his preparedness to meet them halfway. He outlined his philosophy in an address to students at Howard University in 2016:

> And democracy requires compromise, even when you are 100 per cent right. This is hard to explain sometimes. You can be completely right, and you still are going to have to engage folks who disagree with you. If you think that the only way forward is to be as uncompromising as possible, you will feel good about yourself, you will enjoy a certain moral purity, but you're not going to get what you want. And if you don't get what you want long enough, you will eventually think the whole system is rigged. And that will lead to more cynicism, and less participation, and a downward spiral of more injustice and more

anger and more despair. And that's never been the source of our progress. That's how we cheat ourselves of progress.

Moreover, he was able to see that often you could not be 100 per cent sure of your own rightness. More often, the arguments were nuanced and you had to argue your case on the balance of evidence. Consider, for instance, his summation in 2009 of the debate about the morality of stem cell research. 'Those who speak out against stem cell research may be rooted in an admirable conviction about the sacredness of life,' he argued, 'but so are the parents of a child with juvenile diabetes who are convinced that their son's or daughter's hardships can be relieved.' Life is complicated and compromise, he realized, requires you to walk down a two-way street. As he put it to that audience at Howard University:

But listen. Engage. If the other side has a point, learn from them. If they're wrong, rebut them. Teach them. Beat them on the battlefield of ideas ... So that's my advice. That's how you change things. Change isn't something that happens every four years or eight years; change is not placing your faith in any particular politician and then just putting your feet up and saying, okay, go. Change is the effort of committed citizens who hitch their wagons to something bigger than themselves and fight for it every single day. James Baldwin once wrote, 'Not everything that is faced can be changed, but nothing can be changed until it is faced.'

Obama considered the fact 'that the rancour and suspicion between the parties has gotten worse instead of better' over his tenure as one of the few genuine regrets of his presidency. Compromise is, he said, the very essence of democracy and 'the alternative to democracy is always worse'.

GOVERNMENT SHUTDOWN

At its worst, an impasse between the president and Congress can result in a situation where it is not possible to sign off the necessary funding for federal government and its agencies to operate. Under these circumstances, a 'shutdown' ensues where affected areas of government cease operation and staff are put on leave. In 2013, a showdown between Republicans and the president over Obamacare and other specific budget details forced a sixteen-day closure, during which 800,000 federal employees were put on leave and a further 1.3 million worked without knowing when they would be paid. Obama considered the incident 'completely unnecessary'. 'In a normal negotiation you'd sit there and you'd say okay, this is what you want, this is what I want – nobody's going to get one hundred per cent of what they want,' he said. 'What Mr Boehner [Republican Speaker of the House of Representatives] essentially said is, you know, unless I get what I want completely, then I'm not going to reopen the government. Well, I don't understand, and I don't think most Americans understand, why do you need to shut down the government in order to have a negotiation?'

Fighting Prejudice is an Ongoing Struggle

'Now, as a nation, we don't promise equal outcomes, but we were founded on the idea everybody should have an equal opportunity to succeed. No matter who you are, what you look like, where you come from, you can make it. That's an essential promise of America. Where you start should not determine where you end up.'

BARACK OBAMA, 2014

It is a curious feature of the Obama presidency that inequality in the field of race relations seemingly failed to make the significant steps forward that his election, of itself, had promised. If the country had reached a sufficient level of maturity that it could elect an African-American man to the White House, the theory went, then surely the work of Martin Luther King and his colleagues from the civil rights movement was at last approaching full bloom.

But once more, circumstances seemed to conspire against Obama. The financial crisis only served to highlight the economic inequality rife throughout the country and often set along race lines. Moreover, the crisis and a long period of difficult foreign interventions was breeding a sense of isolationism. Mass immigration – legal and illegal – from Mexico became an increasing irritation to some and Islamophobia – with its undeniable racial overtones – rose in the face of emerging international terrorist groups. Domestically, too, there was a surge in recorded police violence against black citizens, evidence of which often circulated on social media. It was altogether a combustible mix that did little to promote cohesion. Obama's default position was to argue that togetherness is inherently better than division. As he put it at Cairo University in 2009: 'It's easier to blame others than to look inward. It's easier to see what is different about someone than to find the things we share. But we should choose the right path, not just the easy path.'

The increase in tensions between the police and the black community in Obama's second tenure was particularly striking. In 2014, for instance, the fatal shooting of Michael Brown by a police officer followed an altercation in Ferguson, Missouri. The event prompted a wave of rioting and social unrest that brought the question of alleged police mistreatment of racial minorities under the microscope. How, many in the black community asked, could such incidents occur in this day and age, and under an African-American president as well? A string of other black deaths at police hands prompted a wave of further protests in the ensuing years. Then, in 2016, police officers were assailed by a black shooter in Dallas, Texas, who claimed to be acting in response to racially inspired police shootings. Five officers were killed and a further nine injured in the deadliest attack on law enforcement officials since the 9/11 attacks. Amid this febrile environment, Obama sought to restore some order and show respect for those on both sides of the divide – ethnic minorities on the one hand and law enforcement on the other.

It was a precarious tightrope to walk. At a NATO conference in 2016, he commented: 'When people say "Black Lives Matter", that doesn't mean blue lives [i.e. those of police officers] don't matter.' But for many within the 'Black Lives Matter' movement (see page 200), such a sentiment was deemed a betrayal from an African-American president. However, that argument was surely unfair, since Obama's position would have become all but untenable – and might well have sparked an upsurge in serious unrest – if he had made any statement that could be deemed as undermining the police. Besides, Obama did urge that the arguments voiced by Black Lives Matter had real basis. Speaking in late 2015, he said that 'the African-American community is not just making this up. It's not just something being politicized. It's real. And there's a history behind it. And we have to take it seriously.'

A little earlier that year, Obama had given a eulogy for Revd Clementa C. Pinckney, one of the nine African-American victims of a racially inspired mass shooting in a church in Charleston, South Carolina. Obama used the occasion to point out the real prejudice that still dogs the nation and which he longs to be addressed. 'Once the eulogies have been delivered,' he said, 'once the TV cameras move on, to go back to business as usual – that's what we so often do to avoid uncomfortable truths about the prejudice that still infects our society. To settle for symbolic gestures without following up with the hard work of more lasting change – that's how we lose our way again.'

At the same time, he was eager to make the case that, while America is yet to resolve all of its racial problems, the progress made since the middle of the twentieth century

THE 'BLACK LIVES MATTER' MOVEMENT

In 2016, over a thousand civilians were killed by police officers in the United States. Nearly a third were black, despite blacks comprising only about 13 per cent of the population. In 2013 the 'Black Lives Matter' (BLM) movement had emerged, originally on social media, in response to the acquittal of George Zimmerman for shooting dead the unarmed African-American teen, Trayvon Martin. It grew into a mass movement the following year in light of a spate of black deaths at the hands of police officers. In its own words, BLM 'is an ideological and political intervention in a world where Black lives are systematically and intentionally targeted for demise. It is an affirmation of Black folks' humanity, our contributions to this society, and our resilience in the face of deadly oppression.'

should not be underestimated. Speaking at the Selma fiftieth anniversary commemorations in 2015, he said:

What happened in Ferguson may not be unique, but it's no longer endemic. It's no longer sanctioned by law or by custom. And before the Civil Rights

Movement, it most surely was. We do a disservice to the cause of justice by intimating that bias and discrimination are immutable, that racial division is inherent to America. If you think nothing's changed in the past 50 years, ask somebody who lived through the Selma or Chicago or Los Angeles of the 1950s … To deny this progress, this hard-won progress – our progress – would be to rob us of our own agency, our own capacity, our responsibility to do what we can to make America better.

Obama was acutely aware that there was much work left to be done to perfect the 'Imperfect Union' that is America. But he saw that bridging the gap required bringing both sides towards the middle. For some, this left him in a hinterland – too 'white' for some, too 'black' for others. To that extent, he was a victim of a specific form of prejudice. Take these words from Stanley Crouch, the writer and commentator, in an article entitled 'What Obama isn't: black like me' from 2006: 'So when black Americans refer to Obama as "one of us," I do not know what they are talking about. In his new book, *The Audacity of Hope*, Obama makes it clear that, while he has experienced some light versions of typical racial stereotypes, he cannot claim those problems as his own – nor has he lived the life of a black American.' Of course, Obama has not lived a typical life. To say that the first African-American president has had a typical life is clearly an absurdity. But as he himself might argue, the 'life of a black man' is simply the life that a black man leads, whatever it may comprise.

Obama did not bring with him the answer to the race relations problem but his mere presence in the White House was a powerful symbol. It cannot be the work of one man though; it must be undertaken by society as a whole. To that extent, perhaps his greatest contribution has been to change the culture. Before Obama, few believed America was quite ready to put an African-American man into the White House. After Obama, we know that it was and a whole new vista of opportunity opened up. As he noted in 2015: 'Americans don't accept a free ride for anybody, nor do we believe in equality of outcomes. But we do expect equal opportunity.'

Guns Do Kill People

'The United States of America is not the only country on Earth with violent or dangerous people. We are not inherently more prone to violence. But we are the only advanced country on Earth that sees this kind of mass violence erupt with this kind of frequency. It doesn't happen in other advanced countries. It's not even close. And as I've said before, somehow we've become numb to it and we start thinking that this is normal.'

BARACK OBAMA, 2016

To many looking in from the outside, the American devotion to gun ownership is a thing of mystery. The Second Amendment to the US Constitution granted the right to keep and bear arms back in 1791, with the Supreme Court subsequently determining that this right is granted in the interests of self-defence. Today, the country has the highest level of civilian gun ownership in the world at almost ninety guns per 100 people. The homicide rate by firearms is easily the highest in the developed world, with gun-related killings making up 64 per cent of all homicides. By comparison, in the UK the figure is 4.5 per cent.

Proponents of gun control argue that the Second Amendment was granted in an era when the self-defence needs of the individual were very different to today. Moreover, arms were mechanically much less advanced. Opponents of reform, on the other hand, defend gun ownership as a sacred right and argue that by surrendering their legally held weapons, the door will be opened to higher levels of violent criminality. It is a debate where compromise has been in noticeably short supply.

Obama made gun control a major feature of his policy

agenda. His time in office was blighted by literally dozens of mass shootings. At least sixteen were so bad that he felt compelled to address the nation in their aftermath. The worst in purely numerical terms occurred in a nightclub in Orlando, Florida, in June 2016 when forty-nine people were murdered and a further fifty-three injured.

Obama has defended the Second Amendment, citing the nation's 'long tradition of hunting and sportsmen and people who want to make sure they can protect themselves'. Aware of alienating the large constituency of pro-gun voters in the country – not to mention powerful lobbying bodies like the National Rifle Association – his proposals for reform were hardly extreme. Speaking in 2008, he laid out his intentions:

I think we can provide common-sense approaches to the issue of illegal guns that are ending up on the streets. We can make sure that criminals don't have guns in their hands. We can make certain that those who are mentally deranged are not getting a hold of handguns. We can trace guns that have been used in crimes to unscrupulous gun dealers that may be selling to straw purchasers and dumping them on the streets.

Yet there would be scant progress in the proceeding eight years, every attempt at reform stymied by Congress. 'Citizenship means standing up for the lives that gun violence steals from us each day,' he said in 2014. 'I have seen the courage of parents, students, pastors, and police officers all over this country who say "we are not afraid", and I intend to keep trying, with or without Congress, to help stop more tragedies from visiting innocent Americans in our movie theatres, shopping malls, or schools like Sandy Hook.'

The unadulterated horror of Sandy Hook had seemed to raise the real possibility that gun reform would finally occur. 'We can't accept events like this as routine,' Obama said in the aftermath of that tragedy. 'Are we really prepared to say that we're powerless in the face of such carnage?

SANDY HOOK

Of all the shooting tragedies that peppered Obama's tenure, none touched a chord with the wider world more than the massacre at Sandy Hook Elementary School in Newtown, Connecticut, in 2012. The murderer killed his mother before taking the lives of twenty children and six members of staff, then committing suicide. The State Attorney's report concluded that the crime was rooted in the shooter's 'severe and deteriorating internalized mental health problems … combined with an atypical preoccupation with violence … [and] access to deadly weapons …'

'These tragedies must end,' Obama demanded. 'And to end them, we must change … Surely, we can do better than this.'

That the politics are too hard? Are we prepared to say that such violence visited on our children year after year after year is somehow the price of our freedom?'

In February 2013 Obama pleaded with Congress to give a chance to reforms including extended background checks and a ban on 'weapons of war'. 'Each of these proposals deserves a vote in Congress,' he argued. 'Now, if you want to vote no, that's your choice. But these proposals deserve a vote. Because in the two months since Newtown, more than a thousand birthdays, graduations, anniversaries have been stolen from our lives by a bullet from a gun – more than a thousand.' A month later and his proposed reforms were once more blocked. His disappointment, even disgust, was evident as he spoke from the White House:

> They blocked common-sense gun reforms even while these families looked on from the Senate gallery … So all in all, this was a pretty shameful day for Washington. But this effort is not over. I want to make it clear to the American people we can still bring about meaningful changes that reduce gun violence, so long as the American people don't give up on it.

Unable to enact the legislation he desired before he left office, gun control reform counts as another of the major disappointments of his presidency.

Be Prepared to Bear the Brickbats

'But we can't expect to solve our problems if all we do is tear each other down … The problem is that this kind of vilification and over-the-top rhetoric closes the door to the possibility of compromise. It undermines democratic deliberation …'

BARACK OBAMA, 2010

As the quotation opposite suggests, even as Obama was striving to foster a climate of cooperation, he knew he had to be remarkably thick-skinned. No major political leader escapes a fair dose of vitriol but Obama at times endured more than might be regarded as his fair share.

Over the years he was pilloried on the basis of his race, over his Christian faith (and perceived lack of faith, too, not to mention sporadic characterizations as a Muslim usually delivered by those who consider the designation an aspersion). He has been accused of being aloof, over-intellectual, more interested in talking than doing. Some have critiqued his reluctance to rush into military engagement, others his interference in the affairs of other nations. He has been attacked for being too pig-headed for his own good or far too willing to compromise with his opponents.

Sometimes, he has raised his head above the parapet to contribute to a debate even as he must have known that he would come under fire. There is perhaps no better example than the speech that he gave to the National Prayer Meeting in 2015. He used the opportunity to push the case for tolerance between the religions, particularly in light of a rising tide of anti-Islamic sentiment in the decade and a half since the 9/11 attacks. He warned his audience: 'And lest we get on our high horse and think this is unique to some other place, remember that during the Crusades and the Inquisition, people committed terrible deeds in the name of Christ. In our home country, slavery and Jim Crow all too often was justified in the name of Christ.' The response was in many ways predictable from some on the Christian right, who interpreted his words either as an unfounded attack upon them or else an act of appeasement in the face of a brutal enemy as epitomized by Al Qaeda and Islamic State.

Obama is too canny to have expected anything less. Yet he still chose to deliver those words. Here is an issue, he seemed to be saying, that goes so deep that the truth must be spoken even if it gives offence to some or sets me up as a focal point of resentment. It is tempting to think that he developed his steely core of resilience during his youth when he so often felt 'apart', so that now he does not require affirmation by popularity as much as the knowledge that he is saying and doing the right thing. He has worn his commitment to particular causes and his determination to see a job through as a suit of armour, off which the poisoned barbs of his enemies usually bounce. 'The one thing I've prided myself on before I was president,' he said in a *60 Minutes* interview in 2011, 'and it turns out that it continues to be true as president, is that I'm a persistent son of a gun.'

THE BIRTHER MOVEMENT

One of the most concerted efforts to undermine Obama was conducted by the so-called Birther movement. Its members alleged that Obama was not, as he said, born in Hawaii but, variously, that he was born in Kenya, took up Indonesian citizenship or else has a dual UK–US passport. As a non-natural-born citizen of the US, the argument continued, he was ineligible for the presidency. It did not escape the notice of many that these entirely unfounded allegations were made against the first president of colour. Among the most prominent of the 'birthers' was future president Donald Trump, who in a televised interview in 2011 expressed a 'little' scepticism as to Obama's citizenship and later speculated that there was something on Obama's birth certificate that he 'doesn't like'. Obama spoke out against the 'network of misinformation' as well as treating the allegations as a humorous sideshow of sorts. The White House ultimately felt compelled to release a copy of his long-form birth certificate to put the matter to rest for all but the most ardent crackpots. 'We do not have time for this kind of silliness,' he commented. 'We've got better stuff to do.'

Seriously, Keep a Sense of Humour

'Six years into my presidency some people
still say I'm arrogant, aloof, condescending.
Some people are so dumb.'

BARACK OBAMA, 2015

Humour, usually of a quite dry vintage, has been another of the key weapons in Obama's armoury as he has dealt with the slings and arrows of life on the political front line. He has been able to diffuse any number of situations, including potentially awkward stand-offs with the press, by suddenly injecting humour into proceedings. His ability to deliver a punchline has served three main purposes: to de-escalate tension, to disarm and to attack.

Many of his best lines have been delivered at the various White House Correspondents' Dinners over the years, at which it has become customary for the sitting president to offer up a self-mocking skit for guests. But he is comfortable using humour in a range of settings, from Twitter to the talk-show host's sofa. For instance, in 2015 he helped diffuse an unfortunate episode in which a fourteen-year-old student called Ahmed Mohamed was arrested at his Texas school on suspicion of carrying a hoax bomb. In fact, it was a simple clock he had been assembling and wished to show to his teachers. Amid claims of racial profiling and institutional Islamophobia, Obama interceded with a Tweet: 'Cool clock, Ahmed. Want to bring it to the

White House?' It was an unexpected flash of good humour in a bad-tempered affair that provided a happy ending to an otherwise unedifying story.

His ability to disarm, meanwhile, is exemplified in a couple of lines delivered several years apart. The first came in 2007 as he made a speech during his run for the presidential nomination. With most of the public still trying to get to grips with the nature of this political newcomer, he offered the following throwaway line:

> The name of my cousin Dick Cheney [George W. Bush's vice president and a man often at ideological odds with Obama] will not be on the ballot. We've been trying to hide that for a long time. Everybody has a black sheep in the family.

Such good-natured bantering ensured many who had been unfamiliar with Obama quickly warmed to him. Similarly, at the 2013 White House Correspondents' Dinner, he addressed the ongoing issue of his race in a way which was both cutting yet without malice. 'I know Republicans are still sorting out what happened in 2012,' he said, 'but one thing they all agree on is they need to do a better job reaching out to minorities. And, look, call me self-centered, but I can think of one minority they could start with. Hello? Think of me as a trial run, you know? See how it goes.'

However, despite Obama mostly mastering the strategic use of humour, there is a theory that one of his jokes had serious unforeseen consequences. Surely the most notorious such instance came in 2011, again at the Correspondents' Dinner, when he went on the attack with Donald Trump. At that time, it should be remembered, Trump was simply a billionaire property magnate and reality TV star. Few then took seriously his sporadic suggestions that he might also have the White House in his sights. Obama took a dig at him in relation to his connections with the Birther movement. Once the White House had produced the president's birth certificate, Trump had attempted to take credit for putting the issue to bed once and for all. 'No one is prouder to put this birth-certificate matter to rest than The Donald,' Obama joked at the dinner. 'And that's because he can finally get back to focusing on the issues that matter – like, did we fake the moon landing? What really happened in Roswell? And where are Biggie and Tupac?' The implication was clear – Trump was no better than a conspiracy-obsessed nutjob. There was more ribbing to come, too, this time about Trump's suitability as a potential presidential candidate:

All kidding aside, obviously, we all know about your credentials and breadth of experience. For example, no, seriously, just recently in an episode of *Celebrity Apprentice*, at the steakhouse, the men's cooking team did not impress the judges from Omaha Steaks. And there was a lot of blame to go around, but you, Mr Trump, recognized that the real problem was a lack of leadership and so, ultimately, you didn't blame Little John or Meatloaf – you fired Gary Busey. And these are the kinds of decisions that would keep me up at night. Well handled, sir. Well handled.

Nor was the humiliation over for Trump, who also had to sit through a number of barbed comments delivered by the dinner's host, comedian Seth Meyers. Among them was this: 'Donald Trump has been saying that he will run for president as a Republican – which is surprising, since I just assumed that he was running as a joke.'

It was widely noted at the time that Trump looked unamused as the cameras fixed on him at his table. He himself would claim that he had had a wonderful night and was merely playing up to the cameras. But the *New Yorker*'s Adam Gopnik had a different impression from his seat a few tables away, as he explained in 2015:

> On that night, Trump's own sense of public humiliation became so overwhelming that he decided, perhaps at first unconsciously, that he would, somehow, get his own back – perhaps even pursue the presidency after all, no matter how nihilistically or absurdly, and redeem himself.

Once Trump had won the presidency, he was a notable absentee from the first two Correspondents' Dinners of his tenure and took to Twitter to critique the event. If Obama's one-liners at Trump's expense seriously contributed to the latter's desire to stand for the office, they doubtless rank in Obama's mind as the worst jokes he ever made.

Obama's Legacy

'We can learn from our mistakes and grow from our failures. And we can strive at all costs to make a better world, so that someday, if we are blessed with the chance to look back on our time here, we can know that we spent it well; that we made a difference; that our fleeting presence had a lasting impact on the lives of other human beings.'

BARACK OBAMA, MEMORIAL SPEECH
FOR TED KENNEDY, 2009

So, what of Obama's legacy? Obama came to office on such a wave of optimism that it would prove all but impossible to meet all the expectations of those who supported him – nor, equally, to dilute his opponents' dislike. As Thomas Jefferson wrote in 1796: 'No man will ever carry out of the Presidency the reputation which carried him into it.'

For some, the frustration of hopes unfulfilled was too much. At a town hall meeting in 2010, for instance, an African-American mother of two named Velma Hart told him: 'I'm exhausted. I'm exhausted of defending you, defending your administration, defending the mantle of change that I voted for, and deeply disappointed with where we are right now.' The following year, Ronald Brownstein wrote in the *National Journal* to give his take on where Obama was losing support.

In 2008, many of Barack Obama's supporters thought they might be electing another John F. Kennedy. But his recent manoeuvres increasingly suggest that they selected another Dwight Eisenhower.

That's not a comment on President Obama's effectiveness or ideology, but rather on his conception of presidential leadership. Whether he is confronting the turmoil reshaping the Middle East or the escalating budget wars in Washington, Obama most often uses a common set of strategies to pursue his goals. Those strategies have less in common with Kennedy's inspirational, public-oriented leadership than with the muted, indirect, and targeted Eisenhower model that political scientist Fred Greenstein memorably described as a 'hidden hand' presidency.

This approach has allowed Obama to achieve many of his domestic and international aims … But, like it did for Eisenhower, this style has exposed Obama to charges of passivity, indecisiveness, and leading from behind. The pattern has left even some of his supporters uncertain whether he is shrewd – or timid.

Obama was given the nickname 'No Drama Obama' for the sense of composure he maintains virtually all the time (although there have been several occasions when he has wept in public, including in the aftermath of the Sandy Hook shootings). His air of intellectualism is also striking. As Michael Beschloss, a specialist in the history of the US presidency, once remarked, 'he's probably the smartest guy ever to become president'. (Although Donald Trump would in turn accuse him of being 'the most ignorant president in our history'.) That he customarily spoke calmly and employed measured arguments, rather than giving himself up to bombast and outbursts of righteous anger, no doubt led some to believe he lacked that wellspring of passion necessary to 'get things done'.

Others, meanwhile, attacked him on policy alone. His handling of the economic crisis was always likely to be controversial. In 2012, for example, historian Niall Ferguson gave this particularly cutting analysis in *Newsweek*:

> Welcome to Obama's America: nearly half the population is not represented on a taxable return – almost exactly the same proportion that lives in a household where at least one member receives some type of government benefit. We are becoming the 50–50 nation – half of us paying the taxes, the other half receiving the benefits. The voters now face a stark choice. They can let Barack Obama's rambling, solipsistic narrative continue until they find themselves living in some American version of Europe, with low growth, high unemployment, even higher debt – and real geopolitical decline. Or they can opt for real change: the kind of change that will end four years of economic underperformance, stop the terrifying accumulation of debt, and re-establish a secure fiscal foundation for American national security.

Obama's presidential record was certainly not one of unfettered success. As we have seen, there were foreign-affairs catastrophes and a lack of progress in key areas that he had put his name to – gun control being a prime example.

He was not able to foster sufficiently good relations with Congress to push on parts of his legislative programme, while others – one immediately thinks of Obamacare – required an exhausting amount of work to see them through. Moreover, his dependence on executive orders and the like leaves some of his best work in a precarious state, since future presidents may attempt to unpick them. In some cases, the process has already begun under Trump.

But his many successes should not be overlooked. He led the country through a time of unprecedented economic upheaval and steered it away from imminent disaster. Obamacare, for all its birthing pains, ranks as one of the great acts of domestic social reform in recent memory. And the Iran nuclear deal and the Paris Accord were both remarkable feats of international diplomacy. Sure, he did not get done all that he had hoped to, but he played the hand he was dealt and came up with more aces than he is sometimes credited for.

It would be remiss to consider Obama's legacy without noting what immediately followed. While the full extent of his legacy will become evident over a much longer timescale, it is an obvious point to make that he was succeeded in the Oval Office by a figure who was in many ways his polar opposite. Donald Trump is, after all, someone Obama suggested was unfit to take the office. His election was a stark statement by the American public, many of whom had wearied of the Washington status quo. From one point of view, it was a devastating rejection of the Obama years – particularly given Trump's pledges to reverse much of his legacy (the Iran and Paris deals, and Obamacare among them).

Yet perhaps the 2016 election might be regarded as more akin to the 1945 general election in the UK, when the great war leader Winston Churchill was removed from office. It was not, in truth, a rejection of the man himself as much as the result of a peculiar set of historical circumstances. A 2017 Gallup polling revealed Obama remained the man most admired anywhere in the world by Americans – ahead of Trump. Obama had held the position for the previous ten years.

There is the nagging feeling that his presidency was one of unfulfilled promise – because of the economy, because of the domestic and political climate, and because of his own occasional missteps too. It may be that it is never regarded as a great presidency – although this author suspects history will judge it more graciously than some contemporary commentators – but Obama still emerges from it with an aura of personal greatness. It might turn out that his greatest contribution to the world is as a touchstone of hope for generations to come. In 2013, Richard Stevenson wrote in *The New York Times* that he was continuing an attempt 'to define a twenty-first-century version of liberalism that could outlast his time in office'.

Intensely relatable at a personal level, Obama is also a symbol. Of social liberalism, of inclusiveness and equality, of thoughtfulness and dignity and determination, of beating the odds. Aside from the policy details of his presidency, his life story speaks of the idea that anything is possible.

In 2008 he campaigned on the slogan, 'Yes, we can.' His presidency seemed to prove, 'No, we can't always.' But as his stint in the White House begins to fade into memory, he remains for many millions around the world a cipher of that continuing message: 'You know what, yes, I think we still can.'

Selected Bibliography

Chait, Jonathan, *Audacity: How Barack Obama Defied His Critics and Created a Legacy That Will Prevail* (Custom House, 2016)

Dionne, E. J., and Reid, Joy-Ann (eds), *We Are the Change We Seek: The Speeches of Barack Obama* (Bloomsbury, 2017)

Obama, Barack, *Dreams From My Father: A Story of Race and Inheritance* (Times Books, 1995)

Obama, Barack, *Of Thee I Sing: A Letter to My Daughters* (Knopf, 2010)

Obama, Barack, *The Audacity of Hope* (Three Rivers Press, 2006)
https://obamawhitehouse.archives.gov
http://obamaspeeches.com/